# Stand & Fall

# Stand & Fall

A Soldier's Recollections of the
'Contemptible Little Army' and the
Retreat from Mons to the Marne, 1914

Joe Cassells

LEONAUR

*Stand & Fall: a Soldier's Recollections of the 'Contemptible Little Army' and the Retreat from Mons to the Marne, 1914*
by Joe Cassells

Originally published under the title *A Record in Action*

Published by Leonaur Ltd

ISBN: 978-1-84677-300-6 (hardcover)
ISBN: 978-1-84677-299-3 (softcover)

**http://www.leonaur.com**

Publisher's Note

# Contents

Foreword                          7

The Left Flank at Mons            9

'The Ladies from Hell'            17

Retire, Retire                    27

Ambulances & Uhlans               35

Bayonet to Bayonet                47

Steel & Teeth                     57

Death at the Wire                 68

Towards Ypres                     78

Scouting in Nomansland            87

Night Patrol                      94

Snipers                           102

Bombing                           109

The Dark Curtain                  117

Buried Alive                      125

Ned MacD's Story                  136

The Black Watch & Me              151

'The Ladies from Hell'            161

# Foreword

From Mons to the Marne lies the bloodiest trail of sacrifice in history. In all the records of war, there stands forth no more magnificent and no more melancholy achievement than that of the British regular army, which bled its heroic way in ever-diminishing numbers from the challenge to the check of the initial German sweep upon Paris. It could not hope for decisive victory; it could only clog the wheels of the Juggernaut with lives and lives and lives, sold bravely and dearly. Before a countless superiority of numbers and an incalculable advantage in enemy preparedness, it could only stand, and fall and stand again, and fall until the end; when the cause of the Allies was saved for the hour, and of French's hundred thousand there remained barely a little leaven of trained men for the British forces then assembling to learn the trade of warfare.

The ablest pens writing of the Great War have paid tribute to this splendid deed which changed the course of its beginning. French's retreat from Mons has been a topic to inspire the highest eloquence of the patriotic historian and the most profound admiration of the militarist. Everything, from the point of the onlooker, has been said of it. And everything that has been said retires into the perspective of the academic, when one reads, in this volume, the words of a trained British soldier who experienced and survived it. For stark and simple strength, for realism of detail, for a complete picturization of the desperate and heroic resistance of the sacrificial army, this soldier's tale is, and will remain, unequalled and unique. This prefatory emphasis is not vain or extravagant. It need not fear the fact that there is but the turning of a page between promise and performance. Here is a writing which is of the war, and therefore differs from all writings which can only be about the war. It conveys to the reader an almost paralyzing sense of wonder at the steadfastness of Britain's military traditions, put to an unexampled test. It shows how marvellously well a soldier may learn his business in advance when his business is to die. Concerning one of the most noteworthy accomplishments of the arms of Britain, there will survive in print no more compelling and convincing narrative than this, the utterance of one whose trade was fighting and not writing.

# CHAPTER 1

# The Left Flank at Mons

For more than two years now, I have been trying to forget those first months of the war. The months when the Black Watch and other regiments of the immortal "contemptible little army" marched into the unknown against the fiercest, most efficient military power the world, up to that time, had known; the months when hidden enemies struck swiftly mystifying blows with strange weapons, the more terrible because we did not understand them and had never imagined their power and numbers.

For more than two years I have habitually sought to keep my mind upon other subjects, yet I can recall those days now in the minutest detail. I can hear the sudden thrum of the masked machine guns like giant partridges drumming; can hear the singing roar of the Prussian airplanes to which, in those days, because of the scarcity of British planes, there could be practically no answer; and I can live again the frightful nights when we made our stand upon the Marne, and, sneaking into German outpost trenches, slew the guards with jack-knives, thrusting gags into their mouths and cutting their throats to prevent outcry.

Those were the days of picturesque and shifty fighting. There was movement, the rush of cannon from the rear, the charges of cavalry, the perils of scouting and patrolling. It was little like the slow trench warfare which followed.

The Black Watch the regiment to which I belong was one of the first to cross the Channel. War was declared August 4th, which was Tuesday. The first-class reservists, of which I was one, received their mobilization orders the next day.

We assembled at Queens Barracks, Perth, the historic headquarters of what we proudly maintain is the world's most famous fighting organization. Twice before, since 1742, the Black Watch had outfitted in Perth to fight in Flanders. Almost constantly since that date, battalions of the regiment have been fighting for Britain in some far-off quarter of the globe. For the third adventure in Flanders, which was to see the existing personnel of the regiment practically wiped out in an imperatively necessary campaign of blood sacrifice, our preparations were brisk and businesslike. Within three hours of my arrival at the depot at Perth. I was one of a thousand men, uniformed, armed, and fully equipped, who entrained for Aldershot to join our first battalion stationed there.

On the thirteenth of August, after a week's stiff training, we boarded the steamship *Italian Prince* and the next day disembarked at Havre.

What awaited us there was much like the reception later given to the first American troops to land in France. What followed was quite different. The American troops, and millions of their friends and relatives, are all wondering what awaits them what war really will be like what they will have to do and the conditions under which they will do it.

It is an axiom of war that the first troops almost invariably suffer the greatest losses.

The first American units to go into the trenches have suffered a low average of casualties. In one respect they are far better off than were the first British and French troops to meet the Germans. They know what they are going up against. Modern warfare is a determined quantity. They know the methods of the men they will fight against and they have allies able to instruct them in the art of fighting as it is practised today.

We had nothing like that. It was as though we were groping in the dark while an unseen foe was striking at us. For days we tramped through France and Belgium hearing the roar of the German guns, feeling the sting of the shrapnel, but not seeing our foes. Then came the shifty, open fighting, now almost forgotten, which will not be resumed until the Germans are on the run. When it comes it will be a welcome relief to the men who have been battling, like rats, in trenches not fit for human beings to inhabit.

Well, to get back to what happened to us, the first "contemptible little army," in France and Flanders.

The 19th of August found us billeted in a town called Boue. We had to remain here a few days because the roads were blocked with transports going toward the front. The entire regiment was allowed to go swimming in a near-by canal and, as my chum and I were dressing, an old Frenchman gave us each a half-franc piece, saying that it would give us good luck and bring us through alive. It was the first money he had made as a boy and he had kept it ever since. The last I heard of my chum was that he had been discharged from active service because of wounds, and so it would appear his half-franc piece really did bring him through, just as mine did me. We left Boue on the twenty-first at three o'clock in the morning, and we marched until three o'clock the next morning. All the time we could hear the muffled booming of the German heavy artillery. It sounded just like the noise they make on the stage when a battle is supposed to be in progress in the distance. It excited the men and buoyed them up wonderfully, but twenty-four hours is a long time to march without sleep, and whenever we halted the men lay down in the mud of the road and lost consciousness but not for long.

Within a few minutes after every halt, the officers would come among us and rouse us, saying that we were badly needed up where the guns were growling. It was hard, tiring work, but it wasn't half so bad as what we got later, when we were retreating.

We didn't know it, but we were on our way to Mons to hold the left flank.

It was during a short halt in Grande Range that we had our first sight of a German airplane. We were billeted in the houses and stables of the village, and every one came running out to look at the plane when the thrumming of the engine was heard. When it was right over our heads it let fly a rack full of steel darts and they came clattering down into the village streets. One stuck into the pavement in front of our quarters. It was so deeply imbedded that not a man in the company could pull it out. (I have seen one of these missiles go right through a house from roof to cellar. They have been known to go through a horse and then bury themselves in the ground.)

These steel darts were from eight inches to a foot long, cut so that they would fall point downward. Dozens of them were contained in a single rack, which the aviator released when he was over his target; the speed of the machine caused them to scatter. They would go through anything they hit, but they were found to be too inaccurate and not so economical as explosives.

After the plane had passed we were rushed to the outskirts of the village, where we began to entrench. By morning, we had nearly finished the shallow trenches which, in that day, were regarded as sufficient protection for infantry in the field. At daybreak our High Command had information that our position along the highway would prove untenable. Wearily enough, we marched to a range of wooded hills where we again entrenched. German heavy shells found us there, so we were compelled to retire to another village, near which we entrenched once more, on still higher ground. The German air scouts were watching us, however, and in this new position a heavier fire from long-range artillery found us.

All of this was on August 25th, two days after our forced march of twenty-four hours.

The weather was extremely hot and we were well-nigh exhausted by the work of digging three sets of trenches. We lay and "took" the German fire. We had already had some casualties, the wooden steeple of the church in the village on our right was hi flames, and several houses had been destroyed by the German shelling and we hadn't yet seen a German, except the airplane scouts. But they were not long coming into view.

As we lay in our shallow trenches, a big shell every now and then falling amongst us, another regiment, retreating under heavy fire, broke into view from the woods, a mile or more hi front of our line. We soon made them out the Scots Guards, hotly pursued by a superior force of Uhlans, and, as the German commander fondly believed, near capture. We, in our trenches, were in a fever to get our fire on the Germans but they were so close upon the Guards that we dared not fire a shot. The Guards, putting up a stiff fight directly in front of our position, checked the Uhlans sufficiently to enable their own organization to continue its retreat, swinging over in the direction of our left flank. This gave us our chance and we poured a hot rifle and machine-gun fire into the pursuing force.

We were in action against the Boches, at last! and,

furthermore, we had the satisfaction of seeing that our fire was effective. The Uhlans, whose attention now was forcibly distracted from the hard-pressed Guards to us, immediately advanced in our direction, dismounting at 1,200 yards distance and returning our fire. Leaving their horses behind a ridge, they crept up on us to within 500 yards.

At this point, a water cart belonging to the Guards, which had been hidden in a thicket, popped out, and was being driven in the direction of their regiment. A party of about thirty Uhlans galloped after it. We turned some of our fire on them. I think they were all toppled over, horses and men alike. Then another party of about five thousand Uhlans made toward us at a gallop and charged, but there were few of them that got to within one hundred yards of our single shallow trench. By this time the Scots Guards had got into position and opened fire on the Boche cavalry.

Three times the Germans tried to secure the water cart, thinking no doubt it was an ammunition wagon. When the cart was about one hundred and fifty yards from our trench the horses were shot down by the Uhlans. One of the men on it was wounded through the arm, and the other coolly filled his water bottle and bathed his comrade's wound, regardless of the Huns who were still peppering away. We shouted to the two boys to hurry and come into safety. The wounded one's answer was:

"Safety be damned! Some of you Jocks come out here and give us a pull with the water cart."

Men of our company, nearest to the cart, asked permission to go to the rescue. Their officers acquiesced and sixteen of them rushed out, cut the cart loose from the dead horses, and dragged it to safety behind the ridge which we were holding. Three of the sixteen were hit. There were especial reasons for this bit of valour. Our own water bottles were empty, our water cart drained dry, and we were choking with thirst.

It was now the time of the Scots Guards to help us. They kept a steady fire on the Uhlans while we retired behind the ridge to fall in on the main road to Hautmont and retreat to the next spot where we could make a temporary stand. While we were falling back to the main road, a man from each section filled three water bottles from the rescued cart. We didn't know when we would get water again, nor how far our tired feet must carry us. In this exhausted state we began the furious fatal struggle against an overwhelming and irresistible enemy which is known in history as the Retreat from Mons. Of that fearful time, I have lost track of dates. I do not want to remember them. All I recollect is that, under a blazing August sun our mouths caked, our tongues parched day after day we dragged ourselves along, always fighting rear-guard actions, our feet bleeding, our backs breaking, our hearts sore. Our unmounted officers limped amongst us, blood oozing through their spats. With a semblance of cheeriness they told us that we must retreat because the Russians were on their way to Berlin and we must keep the Germans moving in the opposite direction. When we got a few minutes' respite there would be an issue of "gunfire" the traditional British army term for tea served out to men in action. It was of a nondescript flavour, commingling the negative qualities of "bully-beef stew" and the very positive taste of kerosene oil, the cooks' hurricane lamps being stored in the camp-kettles during each of our retirements. Invariably and I mean in twenty instances the shells would begin to drop amongst us before we could finish our portions, eating, though we did, with ravenous haste; and when it was not artillery fire that stopped our feeding it would be a charge of Uhlans, compelling us to drop half emptied mess-tins and seize rifles.

We had no artillery to speak of, and very few airplanes. If we had had more of the latter, there might have been another story. The Germans seemed to know every move we made, but we were blind. We dropped into a field and killed a bullock, skinned it and were cooking it. There came the roar of a powerful engine; a German plane circled over us and went sailing back, signalling our position. A few minutes later shrapnel fell among us and we went on, some of the men in ambulances. Those that were killed we hurriedly buried, but there was not time even to put improvised wooden crosses at their heads.

One of our slightly wounded, in the broad accents of lowland Scotch, cursed the Germans not for wounding him, but for knocking over his canteen of tea. A hail of flying shrapnel struck down a cook; the men of his section cursed in chorus for the misfortune which meant that hunger would be added to their other miseries.

Not once alone did we spring up from eating to fight the Uhlans with rifle fire and bayonet. It happened a dozen times. Whenever the Uhlans came, we fought them off, but always we had to retreat in the end, for the German reserves were numberless while ours scarcely existed.

## CHAPTER 2

# 'The Ladies from Hell'

Most of the time while we were dragging our exhausted, diminishing numbers ahead of the German wave of shot and steel, I was on scout duty. For a while, I was "connecting file" between the Black Watch and the Munster Fusiliers who were in rear of us and almost constantly in touch with the enemy. I had more than one narrow escape from capture or death.

On one occasion the regiment had been deployed to beat off a flank attack. When we resumed the march I was sent back to get hi touch with the Fusiliers. My orders were to go to the rear until I got in touch with them. I was proceeding cautiously along the road when suddenly around a curve something appeared before me. My rifle was at my shoulder ready to fire. Then I recognized what had been a uniform of the Fusiliers.

Have you ever read Kipling's "Man Who Came Back"? If you have, you will have a better idea than I can give you of what this human being looked like. His face was covered with blood. One arm hung limply. Just as he made toward me, he fell exhausted by the roadside, like a dog that is spent. Literally, his tongue hung from his mouth. His shoes were cut up and his clothes dangled in ribbons beneath which red gashes showed in; his flesh where he had torn it in the barbed wire fences he had encountered, crossing fields.

I asked him what had happened. His lips moved and his breath came in more difficult gasps, but no word could he utter. I wiped his face, and then I recognized in him an officer who had been a crack athlete when the Munsters were in India and against whom I had competed more than once. I pressed my water bottle to his lips. After a few moments he was able to speak.

"They are gone!" he gasped; "all of them are gone! By God, they died like men; but they died."

"Let me understand you, sir," I begged him. "Tell me just what happened."

"Where are you going?" he almost shouted.

"I am going back to get in touch with the Munster Fusiliers," I said.

"You can't make the journey," he panted. "'You'd have to go to heaven or to hell. They caught them in a pocket. Shrapnel and machine-guns. There are no Munster Fusiliers any more."

He was right, practically. The Germans had caught them between fires and the regiment was cut to pieces.

Helping the officer as best I could, I hurried forward to catch up with my own regiment. When I got in touch with it I left the Fusilier officer with the commander of the first company I met. Then I hurried to the Company commander.

"What are you doing here?" he asked.

"I am here, to report, sir," I said. "There is no use trying to get in touch with the Fusiliers. They have been cut off."

"Your orders were to go back until you got in touch with them," he said gruffly. "Consider yourself under arrest."

A non-commissioned officer and two men, with fixed bayonets, were put on guard over me. I had disobeyed orders, technically, and during those first days in France many a stern act was necessary, for the army had to learn the discipline of war.

I would have been tied to a spare wheel at the back of an artillery caisson, but as they were leading me away I asked to speak to my sergeant. I explained to him what had happened and he told my company commander, who found the officer of the Fusiliers. The latter, meanwhile, had been taken care of by our officers and was now in condition to talk. He spoke to the colonel (Col. Grant Duff), explaining just what had happened and telling him that he had directed me to return to my regiment. I was liberated, but it was a mighty close escape from disgrace, which, after all, is worse than death, especially to a soldier.

After that I was sent out to scout on the left flank with my partner, Troolen, who was of a daredevil disposition and worked in a noisy fashion, and so when I saw something moving in the brushwood on a ridge we were approaching, and heard a sound like the trample of horses on the other side, I cautioned him to remain where he was while I explored it. Troolen swore he could hear nothing and was for muddling ahead and running into anything that might be there, but I was in command and I ordered him to wait. Sneaking from stone to stone and from tree to tree, I worked myself to a little pocket which seemed scalloped out of the crest of the ridge and found the ground there all freshly trampled, with other signs that horses had left it recently. There were no wheel marks, so I knew that it was cavalry, not artillery. From the marks of the iron shoes I could tell that they were of a different type from ours.

Uhlans had been there.

I signalled to Troolen and he joined me. Climbing to the crest of the ridge we saw the enemy in large numbers moving toward the road on which we were marching, and they were ahead of us. As we hurried toward our regiment we heard others in the rear.

As fast as I could, I made my way to the Company

commander and reported what I had seen. Almost at the same moment we were fired upon. The rifle fire was immediately followed by artillery shelling. Patrols on the other flank had made sketches of the country and orders were issued for the regiment to take cover in a gully which was across some fields and the other side of a small woods. The men ducked through a wire fence which was at the side of the road and sections of it were torn to let the combat wagons through.

As we retreated we kept up a steady fire, forcing the Uhlans close to their cover, but the artillery continually sprayed over the field.

Thus began for us the Battle of the Oise.

We had little hope of any support. We knew we had to fight it out alone, and there was little enough ammunition. I was running and ducking for the next bit of cover from behind which I could use my rifle, when a shell exploded behind me. It threw me from my feet but I was unhurt and as I jumped up I heard a crashing and splintering a few feet away. One of the horses on an ammunition wagon had been struck. He was plunging on the ground, terrifying his team mate and kicking the wagon to pieces. The transport officer, C. R. B. Henderson, drew his revolver and shot the animal.

The Uhlans must have had reinforcements for they were getting bolder. The bullets were cutting up little spurts of dust and turf all about us. They were singing overhead like a gale in the ropes and spars of a transport at sea. The Germans were firing at the ammunition wagon in the hope of blowing it up.

I was just about to run for cover again when I saw Lieut. Henderson he who had shot the transport horse walk calmly up (leading his own animal) and cut the dead one from the traces. I didn't care about being killed, but

I couldn't leave this officer, who was standing there as though he were on parade, except that his hands were working ten times as fast as they ever did at drill. Together we got the dead animal free and harnessed the lieutenant's horse to the wagon. We used one of the lieutenant's spiral puttees to mend the cut and broken harness. The driver of the ammunition wagon was holding the head of the other horse, shaking his fist at the Germans, and swearing at them with a heavy Scotch burr.

Men were running past us like rabbits. Some of them were tumbling like rabbits, too, when a steel-nosed bullet found its mark. I saw others stoop, just long enough to get an arm under the shoulders of a comrade and then drag him along. A few lay still and a single look into their faces showed that it would be useless to carry them. The running men dropped behind stones, hillocks, trees anything that was likely to afford cover and stop bullets and their rifles snapped angrily at the Germans whose fire was getting heavier, but who still did not dare an open attack.

At last the harness was ready. The ammunition driver leaped to his seat and the wagon went careening toward the ravine, swaying crazily, with a storm of shots tearing up the turf around its wheels. We needed that wagon badly. In a moment it would be over the crest of the rise and we would be sure of that much ammunition to fight with.

"Get on to the wagon, sir," I shouted to the officer, as it dashed forward; but he did not heed me.

"In a second we shall be where we can fight them off," was all he said.

A Uhlan's horse, with empty saddle, galloped up to us. I seized the dangling reins.

"Mount him, sir," I shouted. He took the reins from my hand and attempted to leap into the saddle. The horse was cut and bleeding, and unmanageable from terror. He backed toward the ammunition wagon, which had not yet made the ridge, dragging the officer with him. I followed.

Just as we thus neared the wagon, a shell exploded close at hand. The wagon humped up in the middle as if it had been made of whalebone. It rocked from side to side, almost upsetting. Then it settled back upon its wrecked wheels. A high explosive shell had struck directly under it. The two horses fell, dead from shrapnel or shock, and the driver toppled from his seat, dead, between them, a red smear across his face.

The small-arms ammunition in the wagon had not been exploded. The doors of the wagon were thrown open by the concussion of the shell, causing the bandoliers of cartridges to scatter. The officer motioned to me to help distribute the ammunition to our men as they ran past; upon finishing this task we joined the last of our party and were very soon over the crest. We had only a few machine guns, but we got them in place. The Uhlans were charging across the field.

A shrill whistle blew. The machine guns began to rattle. Down went horses and riders, plunging about where some of our own men lay. Our rifle fire, too, was getting stronger, better controlled, more co-ordinated. We were sheltered; the enemy was in the open. His artillery was useless, for we were coming to grips. Line after line, they broke into the field, lances set. The horses were stretching out low over the turf over the turf where a moment later they were to kick out the last of their breath, pinning under them many a rider to whom we were paying the debt of the Munster Fusiliers.

A bugle sounded. Those that were left of the Uhlans galloped off. The little machine guns had done their work.

Our attention was then attracted to a heavy fire, directed from some unknown quarter upon a near-by field in which was confined a large herd of light brown cattle, their colour identical with that of our khaki uniforms. The animals were milling about madly; a dozen of them already were down and others were falling each moment. Here was one of the humours of war. We laughed, believing that the Germans were firing upon the dying beasts, mistaking them for us "The Ladies from Hell," as they called us.

The Scots Greys, which regiment had come up at this critical moment to occupy the high ground on our right flank about six hundred yards away, through the fierceness of their enfilading fire, managed to keep the enemy at a standstill and so allowed the Black Watch to retreat to safety.

We owed our lives to kind fate in bringing the Scots Greys to our timely aid, and to them all honour! But for them we should have met the fate of the Munster Fusiliers.

Crawling on their bellies, some of our men went out and brought in those of the Black Watch who were lying wounded. The others we left, for their own men would be there presently. For us, it was retreat again. After traversing ditches, ravines and barbed wire fences, we finally assembled on the road. The artillery was beginning to pound once more. We had to trudge on, watching for the next attack, planting one bleeding foot before another, with nobody knew how many days of forced marching before us marching (so we thought) to let the Russians get to Berlin. I don't think anything else would have induced us to resume our retreat after the brush with the Uhlans.

At evening we found ourselves at the village of Oise about six miles from the abovementioned scene. As we arrived at the bridge over the River Oise, the engineers who were on the other side, and who had fused the bridge, shouted to us to keep back, but our colonel gave us the order to double. We had cleared the bridge by about only two hundred yards, when it blew up into atoms!

After trudging, mostly uphill, in a downpour of rain, we reached a place called Guise at 2 a.m. Here we managed to get some food. I was glad enough to throw my waterproof sheet over me and fall asleep. On being awakened, I felt as though I had slept for weeks, but found it had only been for one hour and twenty minutes. We then received some "gunfire" and our first issue of rum. We resumed the march. On arriving at La Grange, the Camerons, or what was left of them, joined us, taking the place of the annihilated Fusiliers in our brigade.

We were so tired that night that I could have slept on a bed of nails, points up, but we had not been in our billets very long when we were ordered out, as the outpost had reported the approach of Uhlans in considerable numbers.

We were half asleep as we ran down into the street to our allotted posts. One of the first persons we encountered in the town was a Frenchman, raving mad. We asked him what was the matter, but he could not reply. He gibbered like an ape; his twitching lips slavered and foamed. Some of his neighbours took him in hand and led him away. One of them told us his story:

"The Prussians came in here yesterday. There was no one to resist them. They posted sentries. Then those who were not on duty broke into cellars. Casks of wine were rolled up into the streets, and, where squads gathered together, there were piles of bottles. The soldiers did not stop to pull the corks. They knocked off the necks of the bottles and filled their aluminium cups with red wine and white, mixing one type with another, and swilling it in as fast as they could drink. Dozens of them fell in the gutters, drunk. Others reeled through the village, abusing and insulting men and women alike. If a man resisted, he was shot. This poor fellow, whom you have seen, was in his door yard with his wife. A Prussian seized her about the waist. She struggled. He crushed her to him with his brutish arm. His companions, all drunk, laughed and jeered. The woman's clothes were ripped from her shoulders in her struggle. Meanwhile others bound the husband to one of his own fruit trees, so that he could not escape the horror of it. One more drunken, more bestial than the others slashed off the woman's breasts and threw them to a dog. The woman died."

This of itself was enough to have made us rage against the enemy whom hitherto we had regarded as an honourable foe, but it was not all. I, with other members of my own company, came upon a nail driven into the wall of a barn from which hung, by the mouth, the lifeless form of a baby. The child was dead when we found it, but it had died hanging from the rusty nail. I know it had, because I saw upon the wall the marks of finger-nails where the baby had clawed and scratched. And besides, a dead body would not have bled. An officer ordered the removal of the child's body.

I do not tell these things for the sake of the horror of them. I would rather not tell them. I have spent months trying to forget them. Now that I have recalled them, I wake in the night so horrified that I cannot move. But to relate them may serve one useful purpose. There are those in America, as there were in England, who believed that war to repel invasion was justified, but who were not enthusiastic for war abroad. America entered the war after her patience was absolutely exhausted, and Americans should be devoutly thankful that they can fight abroad and not have to endure the presence of a single Prussian soldier on American soil. What we saw and learned in Guise galvanized our weary bodies to new efforts against the vandals whom we were fighting. With clenched teeth and curses we turned to fight again.

The Uhlans got into the outskirts of the town and cut down a number of our men, but, inch by inch, as they drove toward the centre of the village, our resistance became stiffer and stiffer. It was like a nightmare. The charging horses, the gruff shouts of the enemy, the groans of the men who fell beside me, were like their counterparts in a dream. My finger pressed the trigger of the rifle feverishly. Even when I saw the men I fired at topple from their saddles and sprawl on the cobblestones, I had only a dull sense that I had scored a hit.

Just as we were throwing the enemy back in some confusion, a party of British worked round a back street and fired on them from the rear. A second later a machine gun began strewing the ground with horses and men. Squads of them threw up their hands and cried: *"Kamerad! Kamerad!"* which was not a new cry on the part of the Prussians. A young fellow by my side stopped firing for a moment, but the rest of us knew better!

The Camerons had lost a score of men the day before because they had taken the Germans at their word, and, when they went to make them prisoners, a whole company of Prussians had risen from behind the crest to a hill and shot the Camerons down. So bullets from our rifles answered the cries of *"Kamerad!"*

A few of the enemy escaped down side streets, and a number of them remained lying where they had been shot. While we were on our way back to quarters, a Frenchman came up out of his basement and motioned us to follow him. We went into the cellar and found half a dozen Prussians lying there dead drunk. We made them prisoners and sent them to headquarters.

# CHAPTER 3

# Retire, Retire

I had about got settled in the stable where I was billeted, when orders came to "stand to." No more sleep that night. We took the road and left La Grange behind us just as the sun was pinking the sky. It was Sunday, and, although we knew war was no respecter of the Sabbath, we had not been in the field long enough to get the idea quite out of our heads that Sunday, somehow, in the nature of things, was a little easier than other days. When we halted in a ravine at about ten o'clock in the morning, after marching four hours, we thought after all that it was going to be an easier day. I was on outpost duty on a side road a little way from the main thoroughfare we had been following. Suddenly an infernal racket broke out over to our left. First there came a few scattered cracks of rifle fire. Then I could hear clip firing and the rattle of machine guns. I learned later that the Scots Greys and the 12th Lancers had come across about seven thousand Germans resting in a wide gully. The Greys and the Lancers, catching them unawares by cutting down their sentries who had no opportunity even to give the alarm, charged through them, then back again. Three times they repeated their performance, while some of our brigade got on to the flanks and poured in such a rapid fire that the Prussians had no opportunity to re-form to meet each repetition of the attack. The details do not matter, but they made up for the annihilation of the Munster Fusiliers.

In the newspaper accounts of the campaign this incident was described as the "Great St. Quentin Charge," in which, it was asserted, the Black Watch (foot soldiers) participated, holding onto the stirrups of the Scots Greys. This bit of colouring was an inaccuracy. We aided the Greys and the Lancers with rifle and machine-gun fire only. When the firing ceased and the Greys and the Lancers came cantering past, we learned from them the details of the Battle of "St. Quentin."

At nightfall our section was still guarding the road at a point from which a cart road branched off at right angles to the main thoroughfare. It was here that the outpost received instructions in a few French phrases, the main one being *"Votre passe., s'il vous plait."* ("Your pass, please.") This was because the road was open to refugees who were fleeing from the Boches, and who had to show passes before being allowed to go on. The absence of the pass meant that the person would be sent to headquarters for examination. It was quite natural that some of us Scots should find it difficult to make ourselves familiar with these phrases. However, we were all willing to try. One strapping Highlander, weary and footsore but daunted by nothing, practised the phrases dutifully, though the French words were almost lost in the encounter with his native Scotch. We chuckled, but he merely glowered at us indignantly, and then went to take his place on sentry go. Two Frenchmen came along in a wagon. The Highlander blocked their way and sternly uttered what he conceived to be the phrase he had been told to use. The Frenchmen sat mystified. There was a roar of laughter when the Highlander, losing patience, shouted: "Pass us if ye daur!" Then his sergeant came to the rescue.

These two Frenchmen in the wagon were the last refugees to pass. Soon afterward, from my station farther down the road, I heard a clatter of hoofs and caught a glimpse of Uhlans' helmets. I had barely time to pass the word to the man on the next post and to jump behind a log before they came into view. They were riding, full gallop into our lines, apparently having abandoned ordinary scouting precautions in their eagerness to strike where and when they might against our worn and lacerated forces. We, now, had fought so long that we fought mechanically. Over my protecting log, I aimed at the leading horseman as precisely and carefully as if I had been at rifle practice. When I pulled the trigger he tumbled into the road, rolled over awkwardly, and lay still. I did not feel as if I had killed a man. I felt only a mild sense of satisfaction with the accuracy of my aim. Bitter hate for the Huns had sprung in the heart of every one of us after what we had that day seen of their savagery.

I had got my Uhlan at, perhaps, seventy yards. His fall checked the squad's advance for a moment only. The man nearest grasped at the bridle of the dead man's horse but missed it. On they all came, galloping recklessly and yelling, the riderless horse leading by a half dozen lengths. As they rode, they fired in my direction, but their bullets went wide. I felt real compunction as I aimed at the head of the leading horse the one whose rider I had shot down with only a sense of satisfaction. I could hear our men crashing through the bushes by the road as they came to my support. I fired. My bullet must have struck the riderless horse in the brain, for he fell instantly, sprawled out in the path of the galloping Huns behind. The horses of the leaders stumbled over the fallen animal. A rattle of shots from our men completed the confusion of the Uhlans. They turned their horses and galloped away some back along the road, others across the fields. Several fell under our fire; how many we had no time to ascertain.

After that little affair we organized our position for a somewhat better defence.

Leaving a few scouts, far advanced, we stationed our men in easy touch with each other and then cut down a number of trees and telegraph poles and barricaded the road with them. There were sixteen of us in the post near this barricade, concealed from view and able to communicate with each other in whispers. The hours dragged on to midnight and past. We were weary to the bone half dead for want of sleep but we dared not relax our vigilance for an instant.

The surrounding country was dense with woods. The moon was almost new, so consequently the poles were quite invisible a few yards away.

At about one o'clock in the morning I heard something crackling through the brush on the side road. My bayonet was fixed and I was ready to fire. The crackling came nearer. I crept stealthily forward to meet whatever it was. Presently a man stepped into the road. "Halt!" I cried. He halted at once, and gave the word "Friend." It was one of our sentries with a message that Uhlans were coming along the road. Three men were farther down the road; they had hidden so that the Uhlans would pass them, the sentry said.

A section of us concealed ourselves and waited. Presently the Uhlans came into sight, proceeding cautiously. Half of us were instructed to withhold fire until the Prussians should reach the barricade. The remainder began to fire. The horsemen scattered to each side of the road and returned the fire, but as we were not discernible, the shots went wild. I judged that they numbered about fifty. We dropped a few of them. They were becoming enraged their fire ineffective. They mounted; and the leader spurred his horse, and, followed by the others, galloped in our direction. Their carbines spat red flashes into the night. Their bullets were coming closer now, because they could determine where we were lying in the ditches at the side of the road from the flashes of our rifles.

"Will they see the trees across the roadway?" was the thought that darted through my mind. If they should, it would probably be all up with us. As they came very close to the barricade, they did notice it. They made a bold leap across, but having underestimated the number of logs there, they found themselves in great confusion. Some of them were pinned under their fallen horses. At this point, we opened fire, which completed their discomfiture. Above the sound of our rifle firing we could hear the now familiar cry of *"Kamerad! Kamerad!"* It only served to infuriate us and made us shoot all the faster.

This might well arouse against us the criticism of those who never witnessed atrocities committed by the Huns, but you must remember that our blood had not come down to normal from the effects of the sights we ourselves had come across.

At last, we leaped out to make prisoners of the trapped Uhlans. Those who could, bolted back hi the direction they came from, but it was a sure thing that twelve of them were missing when the roll was called.

One might consider that a night's work, but it wasn't.

It was now my turn for sentry go on the main road, which was still open for vehicles of our staff. This was a post where it was thought that, to use an American phrase, there would be "nothing doing"; yet it was here that I came face to face with one of the war's finest examples of Teutonic over assurance boldness that would have been splendid had it not been stupid.

After I had been at my new post an hour, it then being near three o'clock in the morning, a motor car came swiftly toward me. I had been warned that I might expect staff officers to pass, and this, I thought, was undoubtedly some of them otherwise the car would have advanced slowly. I stepped into the road and awaited its approach. As it neared me I saw that the two officers it contained wore the uniforms of the British staff. I could see the red tabs on their collars.

There were two telegraph poles across the road near my post. Remembering this, I showed myself and called for the chauffeur to halt. He checked the car's speed but brought it ahead slowly. I shouted for the countersign. I was waiting for the occupants of the car to give it, intending to explain to them that they would have to stop until I called some one to help me remove the telegraph poles, when there was a sudden grinding of gears and the car shot ahead, full speed. I yelled a warning about the poles but the words left my lips at about the moment when the car bounced over them.

Until that time I had no suspicion that the occupants of the car were not what they seemed. Even then, the manner in which they "rushed" my post seemed to me only due to some inexplicable misunderstanding. But I had marched, and fought, and gone sleepless and hungry until I was little more than a mechanical soldier. I was able to realize only that somebody, for some reason, had ignored my challenge and rushed a sentry post. I swung my rifle in the direction of the car, aimed accurately (in an automatic way), and pulled the trigger. The noise of an exploding tire followed the crack of my weapon. The car skidded, twisted for a moment, and then went on faster than ever.

My shot aroused our outpost. The alarm was given to the first of the connecting sentries and passed along quickly until it reached our company headquarters, on the roadside opposite to a chateau in which Brigade Staff headquarters had been established. Men half awake, tumbled into the roadway preparing to fire on something or somebody they didn't know what. It was useless for the car to attempt to rush the crowd. Again the chauffeur checked it, this time bringing it to a full stop. One of the occupants (who, it will be remembered, were in staff uniform) demanded sharply of the sentry in front of the chateau:

"What is the meaning of this? Are there nothing but blockheads about here? We have been fired on while looking for Brigade headquarters. Somebody should be court-martialled for this."

The sentry saluted them and admitted them to the grounds of the chateau.

Their car had disappeared within the gates when I came running down the road and informed my company commander what had happened. He instantly ordered our men to surround the chateau and rushed in himself, following the car up the avenue leading through the grounds. The "staff officers" had abandoned their car in the shadow of a clump of trees and were seeking to escape over the garden wall when our men captured them. One of them, speaking English without a trace of accent, still tried to "bluff" our men who seized him, and his assumed indignation was so convincing that, but for the direct orders from the company commander, the men might have released him, believing him really an officer of our forces. Each of the two wore the uniform of a staff major with all the proper badges and insignia. It was found that they were German spies with rough maps of the disposition of our retreating forces and other valuable information in their possession. I was informed, later, that they were shot.

Before dawn, we got orders to retire again. It was always *retire retire*. We were ready to fight ten times our number if only we could stop retiring.

Shortly after leaving this position we saw an airplane overhead. A few minutes later shrapnel began bursting in our direction. We scattered to each side of the highway, keeping under cover as best we could.

We marched all day God knows how far and finally, between one and two the following morning, reached a place which we believed to be Pinon.

# CHAPTER 4

# Ambulances & Uhlans

As we neared Pinon, the sound of artillery fire could be heard, and the inhabitants were all leaving the town in any way that they could. Here I saw further effects of Prussian atrocities.

At this spot, a French woman, supporting her mutilated husband as best she could, passed us in a buggy. The sight was awful! His face and body were almost entirely covered with gashes from the Prussians' bayonets. His wife's face was as white as death except where three cruel cuts had laid it open. Neither of this pitiful pair was less than sixty years old. Fine "enemies" for soldiers' weapons!

Beyond this last village we lay in the open for a few hours' rest. We were so utterly exhausted that officers and men alike threw themselves upon the ground and instantly were asleep. My last waking recollection was of the sight of an officer of the guard striding wearily to and fro. He was afraid even to sit for fear sleep might conquer him. And my next recollection seemingly coming right on the heels of the one I have mentioned was of being shaken by the shoulders and having the warning shouted into my ear that we had got orders to force-march instantly.

"They say some of the blighters have got round us by the flank," said the man who shook me. "Make haste!"

We had rested less than three hours. Off we went on another "retirement." This time under the drive of urgent necessity for speed.

We must have marched at an extraordinary rate, because it was not yet noon when we arrived at the outskirts of Soissons. From the high ground on our right flank, we could see cavalry and artillery in great numbers, but whether ours or the enemy's, none of us knew not even the officers. As we arrived in the town we were greeted with artillery fire; then we knew who it was that awaited us.

We got into a lumber yard and returned the fire, but I don't think either side did much damage. Their bullets sang through the lumber gallery. The melody was one that had become familiar to us.

Retreating through Soissons, we kept up a stiff fight, arriving intact at the farther end of the town. Here we came upon fresh and terrible evidence of the ruthlessness and wanton cruelty of the foe which we had first confronted but a few days before, then believing that the traditions of honourable warfare still existed. We came across scores of refugees old men and women who had been beaten and driven from their homes without cause. We had passed the dead bodies of many townspeople killed, seemingly, by artillery fire, yet, in some cases, exhibiting suspicious wounds, as if bayonets or lances had been used. It was not, however, until we were marching through the throng of refugees, outside the town, that indisputable and utterly shocking proofs of the inhumanity of the Huns came to our eyes. In perambulators we saw wailing children with mangled or missing hands. I know that it has been hotly disputed that such dastardly crimes as these were committed by the Germans. I know also that the disputants who contend against the truth of these reports never marched with us the weary and awful miles amid the fleeing and miserable people of Soissons.

These mutilated children I, myself, and my comrades saw. Two at least, I recollect with bloody stumps where baby hands had been, and one whose foot had been severed at the ankle. I saw these things. I saw them; and I live to say that others with me saw them brawny Highlanders whose tears of pity flowed with those of the mothers who wept for heart-break and with those of the babies who wept from the pain of the wounds which had maimed them. Ay, there were witnesses enough; and witnesses remain, though many of the Black Watch who that day saw and cursed the cowardly brutality of the Huns were to lie, but too soon, with their voices hushed for ever, so that they may not speak of it. But we who still live may tell of it and dare a challenge of the truth of what we say! And those who saw, and died paying the toll of that bloody passing from the Mons to the Marne have told it, no doubt, ere this before that Court whose judgment can impose the eternal punishment that the soulless crimes demand.

There were thousands in the unhappy throng of refugees. Some few rode upon hay carts, surrounded by such of their belongings as they had been able hastily to gather. Others pushed handcarts containing their goods and household articles. Most of them however, went afoot, trudging wearily along and carrying what they might. There, in that sickening scene, it was as it is everywhere. The grotesque and the humorous mixed incongruously with the pathetic. For instance: Alongside one perambulator with a wounded child in it rolled another one loaded with huge rings of bread, on top of which perched a parrot, screaming at every one who passed.

One old lady was trudging along carrying a baby which could not have been more than two and a half years old, though the weight of his chubby frame was bending her almost double. I could not speak her language, but I made her understand that I would carry the child a mile or two and leave him by the side of the road. The laughter and baby antics of the child brought a ray of sunshine to our section, and especially to fathers who had left tots behind them in Scotland. About an hour later I came to a group by the roadside, who recognized the baby, and I left him with them, making them understand that the old lady would be along later.

One of the last things I remember in leaving Soissons was an old man who was carrying his furniture and household goods to what looked like a modern dug-out in an embankment and covering it with earth so that it would not be discovered. The boys made a lot of fun of him, but the laugh was not on their lips very long.

We had just reached the top of a hill on the farther side of the city, overlooking the railroad yards and repair shops, when we came into direct view of the German artillery observers, and shrapnel began to storm down among us. It was like the sudden burst of a thunder cloud. There wasn't a moment's warning before the smoke puffs began appearing overhead and the ugly steel splinters and slugs whizzed over our heads.

The regiment deployed in a corn field at one side of the road and scattered, moving some distance from the highway. The enemy continued to sprinkle the corn with shrapnel but we lay flat on the ground until the firing ceased. The company's cooks meanwhile, at some little distance ahead of us, had prepared "gunfire," and the various companies lined up in file to receive their well-earned and much-desired quota of it. As the cooks had to keep ahead of the regiment, there was no time lost in disposing of the tea, and many of the men had to drink it on the run.

A little further on we halted for a few hours' sleep, and at ten minutes to three we found ourselves again on the move.

We marched all that day through a large and dense forest. Now and again we were surprised by occasional artillery shots at the more open sections, but the trees helped a great deal in protecting us from the enemy's airplanes, and proved a hindrance to their tactics. But with the cavalry it was a different matter. Uhlans harassed us every hour of the day. We had only about two machine guns to a battalion, and they were worked so steadily and so hard that they repeatedly jammed. Once we were almost cut off. A party of Uhlans came clattering down on our heels driving the rear guard in on the support, and for a few moments there was what approached a modern barrage fire of artillery on the road in our front. Luckily for us, the artillery fire slackened for some reason and we got ahead before the Uhlans could envelop us.

Later in the day I was serving in the rear guard. Suddenly we heard the roaring of a motor. We took cover at the sides of the road. Our "point" was in the rear, and, if there was anything wrong, we knew they would inform us. The roaring of the motor grew louder. We were so tired that our nerves jangled. I had never felt so jumpy. There it came around the bend with a Red Cross flag flying from it, but it was not one of our ambulances. It had great, heavy, double wheels and there were Red Crosses painted on its sides in addition to the flag flying from the front. Our impression was that it had gone off its course. The chauffeur had released the muffler cut-out and the engine was running very quietly now. A man sitting beside the driver and leaning far out over the side was yelling in broken English that they were lost, and he gesticulated toward the body of the car in such a way as to make us think that he had badly wounded men with him.

We began scrambling back onto the road. Our war was not against the wounded and suffering, so we would let them pass.

Suddenly the ambulance stopped; the sides of it quickly rose; machine guns showed their ugly muzzles.

"*Br-r-r-r t-t-t,*" they began to sputter.

I leaped backward and fell headlong into the ditch. Everybody was jumping for cover. The bullets lashed the road and ricocheted far upon it. Scarcely a man of us was hit, but we were in wild confusion. I cannot describe the scene. No one seemed to think of putting his rifle to his shoulder. The horror of it the passionate anger against such vile trickery drove us into a rage; but for the moment it was an impotent rage. We seemed to be at their mercy.

Then the platoon commander's voice rose above the rat-a-tat of the machine guns:

"Steady, men! Fire at will, but pick your men carefully."

We had heard him speak in the same tone on parade. It brought us to our senses. The edge of the ditch on each side of the road fairly flamed with the sputter of rifle fire. The "ambulance" was riddled. A Prussian officer toppled into the middle of the road. Half a dozen men sprang from the ditch and rushed at him with bayonets. They killed him like a rat. There was no compunction about it.

There was now heard the thrumming of more motors approaching. Round the turn in the road they came. This time it was transports laden with German troops. There was no attempt at disguise with this mob. They thought that their camouflaged battery we ould by now have done its dirty work. Sweating and tugging and straining, we managed to topple the "ambulance" over in the road. The trucks came dashing up as we retreated retreated only to get in touch with our support. The men cheered wildly as two of our own machine guns came up. We turned the wee fellows loose on the Germans gave them a taste of their own medicine.

Some of them came running toward us shouting: "*Kam-*

*erad! Kamerad!"* We shot them down as they ran shot them without hesitation after the dastardly trick they had played on us. Probably they were even then trying another ruse.

The fight surged backward and forward. The Germans tried to press ahead.

Then something happened which we had not expected. A burst of shrapnel sprayed over the Germans. In a few seconds there was another. Then two shells exploded at once three four! A rain of fire, as the French say, was upon them. We were getting support from our own artillery. That was something new and it put heart into us.

The regiment re-formed and proceeded with an orderly retirement, while the artillery, like a barrier of steel, held the enemy at his distance all the rest of the day. We were near to exhaustion and some of the men dropped out of the ranks only to die of the strain. Although our pipers were as weary as the rest of us, they sensed that we needed encouragement, and with great effort struck up a march. Very soon we had left the forest behind us.

It is impossible to describe the effect of the skirl of those pipes that day. It was like a message from Heaven. We had not heard them since Mons, and now they were leading us out of a forest that was a picture of weirdness itself; leading us out into the beautiful open country. What joy we felt!

At this time we were retiring almost directly toward Paris. For seventeen hours we marched with halts only when it was absolutely necessary. We had been in France four weeks, though it seemed like four years.

One of our chief discomforts was the lack of water. Toward evening we halted alongside a cucumber patch. The men simply went wild, running into the field and sucking the juicy young cucumbers. I "drank" twelve myself, but we had not had time to satisfy ourselves when the Prussian artillery got the range again and we had to get out of the field those of us who could. I have heard some "cussing" during my career in the army, but I don't think I ever listened to anything quite like the brand that accompanied our departure from that field.

After marching a considerable distance, we were billeted in barns in a small village. This was a cheering circumstance, as the farmer gave us chickens and allowed us to get vegetables to make up a real warm meal, which I can assure you was enjoyed royally. We expected to stay here some time, so we made for the barns and lay down among the hay.

I don't think you could possibly form an idea of the utter weariness of the men or of the manner in which we were incessantly harassed. We never got a decent chance to eat, drink, or rest. The incidents of the cornfield and the cucumber patch are typical. Many men died of sheer exhaustion. When we entered the barn I was so absolutely petered out that I went to sleep almost before my body touched the hay.

We had been in the barn only about two hours when there was a great commotion. I waked up half suffocated, but I didn't care. Somebody kicked me in the ribs as I was turning over to sleep again.

" The barn's on fire!" he yelled.

There was an odour of paraffin. It seemed that some German agent had started the fire.

Probably it was the owner of the place, using German *"kultur."* Germany had left scores of such spies planted in the country, after 1871.

After the fire in the barn we got a couple of hours more sleep, then moved off again about three o'clock in the morning. We were on the Metz road going east, but did not know it until our officers informed us that we were heading toward the Franco-German frontier. They were ever optimistic and helped to lighten the burdens of men who were on the last lap by carrying sometimes the rifles of four of them at one time on their shoulders. In the afternoon we came to Coulommiers. Most of the inhabitants were leaving, and a herald such as existed in the Middle Ages, was going through the town beating a kettle-drum and crying to all the civilians to take everything they could carry and leave the place. But this herald was a middle-aged woman.

About two o'clock that same day, we were on the banks of a stream and the whole regiment began making preparations for a swim. Some were already in the water, but had scarcely got entirely wet when the German artillery began churning the water with shrapnel. The bodies of many of my comrades went floating down stream.

That night my company guarded a road protected by barbed-wire entanglements and lined with poplar trees; just the kind of road you so often see pictured in France or Belgium. The main body of the regiment was dug in the side of a hill overlooking this road. It was again the luck of my section to protect the road some two hundred yards in advance of the regiment. We entrenched ourselves on each side in such a manner that one could advance within ten yards without detecting our position. We placed a few strands of the barbed-wire fencing across the road a little distance ahead of us.

About midnight, I was awakened by someone tugging at me. It was the sentry. He pointed far up the road, and, as there was a certain amount of moonlight, I could see something moving between the tall poplar trees. He asked me what it was and I told him that it was our cavalry. However, I told him he should inform the section commander; and then I rolled off to sleep again.

Presently I felt a second tug at me.

On looking up I found it was our sergeant; he whispered: "Be ready to spring up at a moment's notice."

The others were already in position. In the dim light I could see the queer-shaped lance-caps that the Uhlans wore.

"Halt! Who goes there?" shouted the sentry.

*"Freunden,"* said a voice in reply.

With that they were almost on the barbed wire, and we greeted them in the way such "friends" should be greeted. There was a tremendous turmoil. All but two fell into our hands. To be exact, fifteen were captured and three killed. Three of the captives were officers.

One of the officers, when searched, was found to have in his possession a novelty mirror with the photograph of a girl on the back. He made no fuss about giving up anything but the mirror. This, however, he insisted upon having back. Finally the examining officer, Major Lord George Stewart Murray, became suspicious and decided that the Boche's sentiment was not on the level. He stripped the photograph off the back. Under it he found a thin sort of skin and, underneath that, pasted to the back of it, a paper covered with writing. He returned the mirror to the German officer, but he retained the paper; and the writing gave the staff much satisfaction.

All night long we were troubled by similar parties of Uhlans. They were evidently feeling out for an attack, but, not being able to gauge our strength, they never made it. Some of our boys crawled out from the trenches to rescue a trooper with a broken leg, and they said that only a few paces away they could not distinguish the trench or tell how many men were there. If the Uhlans had only known the facts they could have swarmed over us. In the morning we collected souvenirs from the field. One of the fellows picked up a lance with two bullet holes clean through the steel tubing shaft.

Our next stop was at Nesles. We drew up alongside a

field of beets just before going into the village, and most of the men fell out of ranks and lay down alongside the road. Some were in the ploughed earth between the rows of beets. The artillery had been firing at us most of the day, but they hadn't found the range. There were some heavy guns hammering at us, as we could tell from the explosions of the shells.

As usual, when it came time for a rest, the Germans began to locate us. One of the heaviest shells I had yet seen exploded in the field and scattered beets all over the surrounding country. A member of our company right near me was stunned for a few seconds.

Before any one had recovered himself enough to go to his aid, he sat up unsteadily, his head wobbling, his face a mass of red. A few yards behind him was his forage cap. He put his shaking hand up to his head; withdrew it, then looked at his fingers which were dripping red.

"Ah weel, lads, Ah've got it noo!" he lamented. "Ah'm sair-r-r-tainly din fur 'cause Ah dinna feel a theng. Ah on'y wesh Ah could 'a got ane o' the deevils tae me credit afore this!"

By this time two or three of us had run forward and were wiping his head and face. There was no evidence of a wound. Then suddenly some one roared with laughter. The man was covered with the red juice of beets and was entirely unhurt. He had only been stunned. This is the way Mars jests. His humour is always mixed with grimness.

We learned that we were to stop at Nesles overnight, and this, coupled with the fact that we had commenced advancing, put new enthusiasm into us.

Before we arrived there were large vineyards at each side of the road leading up a hill overlooking a beautiful little town, on the south bank of the Petit Morin River. We had a few minutes' halt within reach of the lovely French grapes, which hung most temptingly in clusters, so it was quite natural that some of the boys who were extremely thirsty and warm from the scorching sun, should partake of this inviting fruit.

Discipline in the British army is second to none; and we were commanded to observe it strictly while on the retreat. One of our orders was "not to pluck fruit," as it came under the category of "Looting." Very soon the few fellows who had disobeyed that order were rolling on the ground, holding their stomachs. Later we were told that the grapes on both sides of the road had been poisoned by the Germans. This was punishment enough for those who had eaten the fruit, and a lesson that every one of us "took home."

CHAPTER 5

# Bayonet to Bayonet

As we the other scouts and I advanced, firing details, which had been left behind under close cover by the Germans, did a good deal of execution amongst us. The haystacks, particularly, gave us a great deal of trouble. More than once, one of them would be disrupted as though by some sort of explosion from the inside, and machine guns would begin spraying our skirmishing lines. So it became an important part of our scouting operations to search all hay-stacks and farm houses. And continually we were under what, ordinarily, would be termed heavy fire.

The ground over which we were passing had been the scene of sharp fighting, earlier. We came across scores of dead Germans and a few French. In the midst of a field dotted with a particularly large number of haystacks was a farm house. When we were about thirty or forty yards from it and on opposite sides, we leaped up and dashed toward it as hard as we could run. It is a fact that this is the safest way for patrols to approach a house. If any of the enemy are inside, they become excited when they see men rushing toward them and are likely to open fire instead of waiting until the scouts get inside and then killing them noiselessly. Their aim is also more uncertain at a running man than it is at one sneaking along slowly, and, most important of all, whether the scouts are killed or not, the noise of the rifle fire alarms the main body and the party in the house is detected. Troolan (my scout partner) and I arrived at this particular farm house on a dead run without having drawn any fire or detected the least sign of life. We tried all the doors; they were locked. The windows, too, were bolted from the inside. Troolan smashed one in, got inside, and opened the door for me. We searched the building rather hurriedly and discovered no sign of any one having been there. Just as we were going out, I had a premonition that I ought to look further.

"Wait outside and watch," I said to Troolan, "and I will take another look around."

He posted himself outside. Very cautiously I stepped down the cellar stairs. The boards seemed to squeak and groan like a lumbering farm wagon. It was dark as pitch, but I did not dare to make a light. It would have been fatal if any one really was lurking there. Something scurried across the floor. I felt the hot blood surge under my scalp. For a second I expected to see a red flash in the utter darkness and feel a bullet smash into my body. Then I discovered that it was only a rat.

I thought I heard breathing. I stood stock still, and strained my eyes on every side till they ached as if they would burst from their sockets. I was trying to catch the reflection of some stray beam of light from the eyes of a man or the barrel of an automatic, but I do not believe that so much as a pin point of light was diffused in that whole black pit. Suddenly I almost laughed aloud, although I knew that to do so might mean instant death. The breathing that I heard was my own. Cautiously I thrust out my foot to descend another step.

There was a shout outside.

"Run to the door quickly," Troolan was yelling.

I leaped up the stairway regardless of what might be behind me and dashed toward the kitchen door to get outside the house. Just as I did so, I saw a shadow flit along the ground past the kitchen window. Guessing where the man must be who cast it, I fired through the wooden wall of the kitchen at about the height of the average man's breast. Then in a couple of bounds I was outside. There stood Troolan looking very much surprised and grieved when he saw me. His rifle was half drawn up to his shoulder, and he was in the attitude of getting ready to fire.

Perspiration broke out on my forehead. I realised that the shadow had been Troolan's and from the look of him I had come very nigh to killing him.

"What the h— was that for, ye muckle galoot?" he threw at me.

"I saw a shadow," I said, "and let drive."

"Ye're an auld wife, that's what ye are," said Troolan disgustedly, "a'firin' after shadows."

"Never mind now," I said, "what did you see?"

"I saw a big boche," said my scouting partner, "or, at least, I thocht I did. Maybe I've been takin' you fur him the same as you did me."

"Maybe," I said, "but the best plan is for you to watch this house while I go and report."

"All right," said Troolan.

I started away. I had not gone a dozen paces when I heard scuffling behind me. I turned round and started to run back at the same instant. What I saw lent speed to my feet. The helmet of a German officer was just coming through a window. Troolan, who had evidently been concealed from the German's view, was aiming a blow at his head with the butt of his rifle.

As usual, Troolan had lacked finesse. He had rushed so clumsily to the attack that both the officer and I had heard him. The German dodged just in time to evade the blow, and Troolan's rifle banged the window sill.

How the boche did it, I do not know, but it seemed as though he was propelled by strong steel springs under his feet. He fairly shot out of the window like a dart from a catapult and landed on Troolan's neck. Both men went down. I dared not fire. They were rolling over and over one another, kicking and striking with their fists. The boche was fouling Troolan in a way that would be prohibited in wrestling. I jumped into the fray and tried to find the German's throat, but the men were so entwined that it was hard to get a hold on him. Suddenly a heavy boot struck me in the pit of the stomach, and I rolled over and over to find myself gasping for breath a dozen feet away.

Painfully I got up and staggered toward the struggling men, but I was too late to be of any use. After a particularly frantic struggle Troolan managed to get on top of his adversary, with his right arm free. His mighty fist came smashing down full in the other's face. The German staggered to his feet, but Troolan leaped clear of him, seized his rifle, and, this time, brought the butt down with a thud on the other's skull. Then Troolan burst into some of the most profane Scotch it has been my doubtful privilege to hear.

"What are you cursing about?" I asked him.

"I want to mak shair that Deevil's deed!" he said.

Later that day we were relieved by other scouts.

Toward nightfall troops began to arrive on either side of us in great numbers, and dispatch riders with various insignia continually dashed up on their speedy motorcycles to our brigade headquarters. Everyone realized that we must be approaching something big, for previous to this we had been fighting, for the most part, isolated engagements. As a matter of fact, it developed that we were preparing for the Battle of the Marne.

We remained at this spot all night. At dawn, orders were given that we were to take the high ground the Germans were occupying a few miles ahead of us. Our brigade marched in skirmishing order, followed by the cavalry and artillery. We passed scores of dead some French but the majority German. Dead horses were intermingled with the bodies of men.

We were under heavy shell fire until we descended into the shelter of a gully. Here we met a few of the French Chasseurs. Four or five farms were clustered together, and the sights we encountered in the yards and on the roads were the worst we had yet seen. Pools of congealed blood; bodies of dead soldiers partly covered with sacks and straw; the barns so filled that the feet of dead men were protruding. The Chasseurs appeared very pale and silent.

The ridge was densely covered with hazelwood. We got the command to fix bayonets and extend into skirmishing formation. The Black Watch with the Camerons were to take the ridge, while the Coldstreams and Scots Guards were to be in reserve.

An incident occurred during the ascent of the ridge which illustrated the reckless, devil-may-care spirit of the men in our battalion in a way which impressed even me. The front-line men came upon a lot of blackberry bushes. They began plucking and eating the berries, shouting gleefully to one another to signal the discovery of an especially well-laden bush. Until the officers sternly warned them of the peril they invited by such noise and incaution, you would have thought they were schoolboys on a lark.

I was one of the scouts sent up the ridge to try to locate the position and number of the enemy and report at once. Wriggling along on my belly like a snake, I made my way foot by foot. I could hear our fellows shouting, and it rather disconcerted me as I felt they would attract the enemy's attention, but I continued on my way nevertheless.

I never knew that so many sharp stones could be scattered in so short a distance. It seemed as though some of them were forcing themselves clean in between my ribs.

Presently I came to a hastily constructed barbed-wire entanglement at the edge of a thicket. Ahead of me was a clear rising space of about fifty yards which did not show from below. Beyond this was a plateau. Before advancing farther I peered through the thicket and scanned the crest.

Suddenly I heard a familiar, unmistakable rattling. It was the opening and closing of rifle bolts. My skin prickled all over. I knew that it meant troops getting ready to fire and I had no doubt the Germans had discovered me and were preparing to shoot. I wriggled backward a few feet into the thicket, expecting every second to hear the crash of a volley and to pass into oblivion. But the crash did not come. Evidently they had not seen me.

Under cover of the underbrush I crept forward again until I could see the helmets of German troops in the woods atop of the ridge. They outnumbered our troops. I crawled to the left until I came to a point where I could command a view of the crest, where they were in waiting, but apparently unaware of our near approach. I crawled back until I was out of sight. Then I leaped to my feet and ran as if I were once more on a cinder track in the old barrack days. Brambles tore my hands and face and lacerated my bare knees, but I did not heed them.

I had seen enough, and the sooner we could make the attack the better. Besides, they might even yet see me, and I preferred the scratching of brambles to the bite of a steel bullet.

In safety I got back to our lines. The boys could see from my excitement that something was up.

"Did you find them, Joe?" they shouted.

"Where is the adjutant?" I demanded. Somebody told me, and I hurried to him.

"How many of them are there?" he asked when I told what I had seen.

"All I can say, sir, is that they outnumber us and are waiting," I answered

Orders were given for an immediate attack.

I went forward again, but this time in my own place in the company, with men either side of me, and with real business ahead. We made our way in silence through the woods toward the terrace. Still the Germans did not fire. We wondered whether they were really unaware of our approach, or, just holding their fire for close range? This was the first time we had been in a big attack of this kind and we knew that bayonet work would be the end of it.

The answer to our questioning soon came. It was in the form of a burst of fire from the ridge above us. Twigs fell all around us and here and there a man dropped too.

We could not do much in the way of returning the fire, for we had not yet reached the open. The blood was pounding through my arteries. I felt much as I used to before the start of an important race. The second platoon to my right went forward, while our fire covered their advance. Crouching low, the men dashed on at full speed. Here and there one of them toppled backward. Then the platoon nearest to us advanced. It would be our turn next. We ceased firing and prepared to rush. Our lieutenant looked at the commander, whose whistle had just blown a shrill blast. He signalled for us to go forward.

Like one man, we leaped to our feet. The thin line swept out onto the open terrace. Each man had but one friend then, his rifle with the bayonet fixed.

We had arrived at the point where I had previously

encountered the barbed wire. Throwing ourselves flat on the ground, we returned the enemy's fire. After cutting the barbed-wire, we awaited orders. The word came to charge. With one mighty shout, we made for the crest. When one goes out with the bayonet he goes to kill or to be killed, but with the former in mind.

The German fire thundered out as though it had been tripled. The trees and bushes were cut as by scythes, but they were only shooting in a direction they could not see us clearly. Up, up we went. Loose stones rattled under our feet, and went tumbling down the slope, but we picked ourselves up and pushed always forward and upward. At last we saw the Germans who were firing at us over their trenches. Our men were yelling like demons.

Then the German fire stopped as though every man had, on the instant, been struck dead. An instant later, they leaped out of their trenches, with bayonets fixed, and dashed toward us. Every man among them looked a giant. One of our boys was ahead of all the others. He was a bow-legged little fellow, and, even at that moment, he looked ludicrous with his bare knees and kilts. A big German was over him. The little fellow seemed to drop his rifle. He had caught it in both hands, close under the handle of the bayonet. He straightened up, heaving his shoulders, brought up his forearms with a jerk, and the steel blade drove through the soft spot in the German's throat just under the chin. The Prussian's last cry was drowned by the fierce yell of the little bowlegged man. It was the spirit of the bayonet which made him yell like a savage.

There was no time to see what was going on around me any more. We were fighting knee to knee. I can but faintly recall the actual close fighting, but I seemed to make good use of my bayonet. Sometimes I was knocked off my feet, but the next instant I was up again. I was not thinking of what might happen to me. It was fight, fight, and keep on fighting. One seemed imbued with a superhuman strength.

One of our boys seized a German's rifle, and wrested it from him by a trick which seemed to break his arm. A little farther away two Germans were rushing upon one man. Mechanically, I leaped into action. The butt of my rifle felled the nearest boche. Somebody knocked the rifle out of my hands. Somehow I ducked a thrust made at me and ran in on the German who made it, and smashed my fist on the point of his jaw.

They began to waver now. They did not seem to care for our company with our kilts and our steel we whom they later learned to call the "Ladies of Hell." (Because of our kilts.) At last they broke and ran. We were after them. A machine gun rattled away at the head of a path down which some of our boys were dashing. It almost wiped out B company before we could silence it.

Just over the crest of the ridge we came upon their combat wagons and a field gun. Three men and an officer were trying to save the gun. The men who were hitching the horses to it broke and ran. The officer did not hesitate a second to shoot them in the backs. Then he fell with one of our bullets through his head. We captured the gun.

By this time I was regaining my proper senses. A feeling of exhaustion seemed to envelop me; my legs wobbled. Then I dropped to the ground. Every bone, muscle, and nerve ached, and I felt as though I had just been through a tough wrestling match.

When we had counted up, we found that two company officers, Captain Drummond and Captain Dalgleish, had been killed. We picked up about fifty German rifles and broke them over the trunks of trees. Our casualties were one hundred and fifty killed and only God knows how many wounded.

Our prisoners amounted to about one hundred and forty. Among them was a man who had worked in London as a watchmaker. In very broken English, he asked if he could get his job back if he were sent to London. We told him that he would get a job all right, but that somebody else would see to the watchmaking.

After capturing the crest, upon looking from the far side, we could see great numbers of German cavalry and infantry in retreat. The plateau was strewn with I should judge about five hundred dead bodies of the enemy. Their horses that had been wounded were left behind, left to die. We let go a few volleys of long-range fire to hurry the boches on their way.

## CHAPTER 6

# Steel & Teeth

We had very little rest after the fight I have just described. We were getting down to the real business of war. It was fighting, and not the incessant retreating, which had been sapping the life out of us for weeks. You must remember, also, the weight that each man carried during all those long wearisome retreats. Each of us had his heavily plaited kilt; his pack containing great coat, flannel shirt, two pairs of socks, waterproof sheet, extra shoes, and towel; his canteen, rifle, entrenching tool, bayonet, and ammunition the whole totalling ninety pounds weight.

Immediately after the fight, in shallow, narrow trenches, we began to bury our dead. Before the work was finished, a detachment of Uhlans fired on us, but one of our companies drove them across a rivulet and over the crest of the next ridge.

One of our pipers, Dougall McLeod was His name had lost his chum in the fight. McLeod was a sentimental sort of chap, with little heart for the work of killing. He was sitting on the ground fastening together a couple of strips of wood to make a little cross for his chum's grave or rather his chum's share of the one long grave. The tears were trickling down his grimy, bloody cheeks, and he wasn't ashamed of them, nor of the furrows they cut in the caked dirt. It was just before he finished his work that the Uhlans opened fire. McLeod threw the loose pieces of the cross to the ground, and sprang to his place in the firing line. I had never seen the passion of hate in his eyes before. All that the Germans had made him suffer had never aroused him, but now that they interrupted him in the work of making a homely mark for his friend's grave, he was fired by the will to kill. I was only a few paces from him in the firing line, and, with the tears still streaming down his face, I could hear him mutter every time his rifle crashed: "Damn you! You will, will you?"

We again took to the road.

All that day we marched under occasional shell fire. Along the sides of the roads, we passed the wrecks of scores of German combat wagons and supply trains. Sometimes there was a field piece amid the debris. Toward evening we heard terrific firing on our right, but we were not called to enter the engagement. Later we learned that a French division had been pretty badly cut up in running the boches out of a strong position.

Their wounded passed us on the road. You cannot imagine a more pitiful or a more noble sight. Limping along, supported by their comrades, came scores of men, whose every step was costing them agony but who smiled at us as we cheered them. Straggling down the road, as we swung along, came groups of wounded, each supporting the other as best he could. In one case in particular, a man who had been badly maimed and was using his rifle as a crutch, was also supported by a comrade who had been blinded. If there had ever been doubt in our minds as to the mettle of our allies, it was dispelled now, as the lame and the blind hour after hour filed past us.

We billeted that night at a place, the name of which sounded like Villers. I remember that a detachment of

French were there before us, and a peasant pointed out to me a row of trees where they had hung fifteen Germans captured there, because, when the Uhlans had taken the town fifteen of them had brutally assaulted and outraged a farmer's wife and his daughter, twelve years of age. The ropes were still dangling from the trees.

Volunteers were asked for, to go down and get the mail. Practically everyone offered his services. To get mail from home gave the same sensation as scoring a victory, and we were all eager to do our bit. This was about 10.30 p.m. and the rain was coming down in torrents. About two miles behind us lay the mail strewn around the road. The ambulance carrying it had been struck by a shell. Our volunteer mail carriers gathered the letters up, and, needless to say, there was much excitement among us on their arrival. Nothing else was thought of for the moment except the news from home.

The next few days were uneventful. Toward evening on the thirteenth of September, I was scouting on our left flank. The German heavy guns had been keeping up a steady searching fire all day, but little damage had been done.

I had got so accustomed to the roar of the explosions that they did not bother me very much. After a while a man gets so used to the sound of a shrieking shell in the air that he can tell by instinct when one is coming his way in time to throw himself flat on the ground. I had not yet reached this stage of proficiency.

A shell did come my way. How close it came I will never know, because all of a sudden I felt as though my head were bursting. I seemed to be tumbling end over end and being torn to pieces. My ear drums rang and pained excruciatingly. I thought to myself "I am dying," and I wondered how I kept feeling a sort of consciousness although I must be already torn to bits.

Then I found myself sitting up on the ground with a man from my patrol supporting my head.

Now, this is the strange thing. I was instantly and absolutely oblivious when the shell exploded. All the sensations I have described came when I was recovering consciousness.

Surgeons have told me since then that they were exactly what the shell caused when it exploded, but that my brain did not register them until my senses returned. My clothes were scorched and even my hair was singed. I do not know why I was not killed, but in a few hours I was ready for duty once more. The man who picked me up said that the shell had burst some little distance overhead. If it had struck the ground close to me, it would doubtless have sent me "west."

The game had now been turned about. We were the pursuers. Most of the fighting was between the enemy's rear guard and our contact patrols until we reached the Aisne. The Huns crossed the river, but they blew up the bridges behind them. The last of the retreating troops were scarcely across before the detonators were set off.

We were held up for a while on the Aisne while our engineers constructed pontoon bridges. The Germans had the range, and they almost wiped out our entire battalion of engineers before our troops could cross.

I saw a working raft swing out into the river with about twelve men on it. A single burst of shrapnel exploded in their midst and there wasn't a man left standing. One of them crawled to the stern and began pushing the raft toward shore with a pole but he was so weak that the current kept swinging him down a stream. A sniper got him.

The raft was drifting away. Nobody expected to see the men on it again, but, in the face of shrapnel and a nasty fire from snipers, three men, stark naked, jumped into the stream and struck out for the raft. The water around them was whipped by bullets, but our boys located the snipers and got the range and quieted them. The first man reached the raft. His hands were over the edge. He had just pushed his head and shoulders over the side when a rifle snapped and he slipped back into the water; then I saw the German who had fired at him topple out of a tree. A dozen shots must have struck him. The two other swimmers were alongside the raft now and climbed upon it. I could see that one was bleeding at the shoulder. Our men pulled the wounded man upon the raft, and brought it to shore. Their heroism saved the lives of five men who other wise would have drifted away and probably died.

Soon our own artillery began to locate the German guns, whose fire diminished. Then our infantry began to cross the river at a dozen points. On the opposite bank was a village by the name of Bourg. Up and down hills we worked our way, forcing the enemy off the ridges. The details of the operations would not be of interest. We wanted to close with the bayonets, but the boches weren't ready for that, and they dropped back foot by foot, keeping up a hot fire.

On this side of the river were numerous stone quarries, and in these we found tons and tons of ammunition for the heavy German guns. The type and manufacturers' marks showed that some of it was made as far back as the Franco-Prussian war. It had been lying in caches in the quarries for years, the Prussians having bought titles to some of the land through spies who posed as Frenchmen. They had been making use of this ammunition against us. It shows how long ago the war was planned and by whom. In some of the quarries we uncovered re-enforced concrete fortification and emplacements for cannon.

Our commander, Colonel Grant Duff, was in the thickest of the fighting. I saw him distributing bandoliers of ammunition along the firing line. His men tried to make him go to the rear, but we were having a tough time to keep fire superiority, and we needed every man in the line. Suddenly Colonel Duff staggered and slouched forward on his hands and knees. The bandoliers he was carrying, scattered. Several men rushed to him but he got to his feet himself and ordered them back to their posts. An ugly red stain was spreading over his tartan riding breeches and leggings, but he staggered onward with the ammunition. He had not gone a dozen steps when both his arms flew up into the air and he fell backward. This time he did not move. He had been shot straight through the heart, and another commander of the Black Watch had gone to join the long line of heroes who had so often led this regiment to victory.

Many of our company commanders were picked off by the enemy because of their distinctive dress, their celluloid map cases affording excellent targets.

My memory of this fight is somewhat fragmentary. There are phases which are all but blanks to me. Others stand out with startling clarity.

We were advancing in skirmishing order through a wood. A pal of my old athletic days, Ned McD, fighting a few yards from me in our scattered line, fell with a bullet through both thighs. I made him as comfortable as I could in a nook about twenty paces back from where our men, lying on their stomachs, were keeping up a steady rifle fire through the underbrush. I had hardly returned to the line when the whistle of our platoon commander sounded shrilly, and we were ordered to retire to the farther edge of the plateau, where our men could have better protection from the enemy fire. I hurriedly placed McD under the edge of a bank, where, at least, he would not be trampled on by men or horses.

"Don't attempt to leave the spot, Ned," I said. "I'll get back to you to-night if there's an opportunity."

The chance did come, but when I reached the spot he had disappeared. Our subsequent meeting the story of which I shall tell is one of my few agreeable recollections in the train of the tragedy of our campaign.

But to go back to the fight.

Soon after leaving the spot where McD lay, I joined in a charge on a line of hidden trenches. We were upon them, and it was steel and teeth again. I saw an officer run in under a bayonet thrust, and jab his thumbs into a German's eyes. The boche rolled upon the ground, screaming. How long we fought, I do not know. When it was over we began to pick up the wounded. It was night. The Prussian guns were still hammering at us, and some of the shells set fire to a number of haystacks in the field where we had crossed the open. It was Hell. In the red glare of the fire the stretcher bearers hurried here and there with the dying, while others who had been placed behind the hay-stacks for shelter burned to death when the stalks caught fire. The few who could, crawled away from the fire. Those of us who were able to do so, pulled others to safety, and many a man had his hands and face badly burned, rescuing a helpless comrade.

The next morning we went at them again. In the first rush, I felt a sudden slap against my thigh. It did not feel like anything more than a blow from an open palm. I thought nothing more of it until after the fight, when some one told me I was bleeding. A bullet had struck the flesh of my thigh. The slight wound was dressed at the regimental station, and I was ready for duty again.

That night I was assigned to outpost duty between the lines. The German artillery had so covered the roads and the bridge, that for two days the supply wagons had been unable to come up. I was almost starved. My stomach ached incessantly from sheer hunger and I was weak from the bleeding of my wound. It seems terrible, looking back at it, but, during the night, while my partner watched, I crawled out and searched the dead for rations. I found none. Fifty paces from our post lay a dead artillery horse. We had to eat or drop. What could we do? Wriggling on my belly like a snake, I drew myself toward the smelling carcass, cut off enough with my jack-knife to do the section, brought it back, and we ate it.

There followed days of lying in the trenches. Every time one of us showed a head above the surface of the earth a single shot would ring out, and more than once it accomplished its mission. Two or three times I almost caught it myself. At last I made up my mind that the sniper must be in a sugar factory building which showed clearly above a ridge on the right front of our position. Jock Hunter and I volunteered to go there and investigate. Working our way under cover of a wooded patch, we reached the factory yard where we encountered an old Frenchman who seemed to be the owner of the place.

"What do you want?" he demanded.

"Have you seen a sniper anywhere about here?" I asked.

"No," he answered in a surly manner, "and you get out of here."

"We'll get out," I retorted, "and you'll get with us."

I searched the factory building from cellar to roof but wasn't able to discover anything incriminating. I didn't know much about sugar factories, but there was a lot of machinery in the place that didn't look to me as if it had anything to do with sugar.

Back to our lines we went, with the supposed Frenchman making a lot of noise, but walking about two inches in front of the points of our bayonets. When he was searched we found notes to the value of fifteen thousand francs sewed in his clothes, but most important of all, there were papers upon his person which showed that he was a German spy left there by the Prussians in 1871. He held title to many acres of land, including some of the quarries where shells had been hidden.

I told the company officer of the suspicious looking machinery in the factory. He sent us back there with a subaltern of the engineers. The three of us approached the building by different routes. Suddenly, from a narrow window in the tower of the structure, a rifle cracked, and I saw the subaltern duck behind a bush. Hunter and I each began to run toward the factory. *Zip!* A bullet whistled past my ear, and a few seconds later Hunter was fired at.

We all reached the place together. As the firing had been from the tower, we hurried to the upper storeys, but the subaltern saw at a glance that the machinery I had noticed was a wireless plant. Afterward we found that the numerous "lightning rods" on the factory were in reality wireless antennae. We went to the top of the tower without finding a single soul, but in a little room in the cupola, there were a few breadcrumbs scattered over the floor. A corner of the linoleum covering on the floor of this room looked a little uneven. The subaltern posted each of us. in a different corner with orders to fire three rapid rounds from our rifles into different points of the floor. He himself was to discharge his revolver in a like manner. At his signal we all opened fire, splintering the floor in several places. Then we heard a groan.

"Come up here!" called the subaltern, in English. There was no answer. He repeated the command in German. Very slowly the linoleum in the corner of the room where it was uneven began to hump up. We all stood ready to fire. A trap door was lifting.

Presently the corner of the floor covering was pushed back completely and a man's face appeared. It was a very white, drawn face, and, as the shoulders rose above the floor level, we saw that the man had been struck by at least one of our bullets. His left arm hung limp by his side. We patched him up.

The officer told Hunter and myself to cut all wires, which, after some search, we found had been laid at the bottom of the walls and cunningly concealed by the grass. Then we took our prisoner back to our lines. An hour later our howitzers had demolished the factory. Up to this time, the boche artillery had been planting one shell after another on our positions, no matter how often we shifted. After the factory was destroyed we made one more move and no shells found us.

We dug ourselves into the ground, and the almost continual rain made mud holes out of the trenches. Our force was not large enough in those days to allow of the elaborate system of supports and reserves that exists to-day. The men in the firing trenches had to stay there, and there was no going back into bomb-proofs for a rest. At night we lay down all in our muddy clothes with a waterproof sheet beneath us and our greatcoats around us. The sheet didn't do much good, because after lying in it for a while, it got pressed down into the mud and slime, which came all over the edges. Every one had a cold, and many of the men suffered from rheumatism, but no complaints were heard. It is only when things are going smoothly and "fags" are lacking that the British Tommy kicks.

Owing to the lack of supplies, the issues of cigarettes were so few and far between that the dry tea that was sent up as part rations was used to make "fags." Tommies would roll the tea in paper in the form of cigarettes and smoke it. As much as five francs would be offered for one "Woodbine" when our supplies were exhausted. A "fag" was a most precious thing, and guarded jealously. A fellow would get into a corner, take a couple of puffs, "nip" it, then hide it away in a safe place on his person for fear of thieves in the night!

In one instance, I watched a scene that would have brought forth laughter as well as pity from a civilian. One Tommy was observed in a corner finishing a half-inch butt, holding it by a pin which was stuck through it. Three others immediately pounced upon him and his treasure. After a short argument they formed a truce in the following manner: each man in rotation was to take one puff. A cockney with a Walrus moustache was last on the line, and with great sadness on his face and a sob in his voice said: "Blimey! w'ere the 'ell do *I* come in?"

Out in front of our trenches the mud was full of the bodies of the dead mostly Germans, but a few of our men. At night, we went out to bury them, but the enemy fired on us, so we had to leave them there. The wind was blowing our way, and they knew the odours of the battlefield were as hard for us to bear as was their artillery or rifle fire. This scheme they had learned from the Russians, who practised it during their war with Japan.

# CHAPTER 7

# Death at the Wire

Our trenches were pretty effective against rifle fire, but we had not yet learned to make them deep and narrow enough in proportion to protect us against shrapnel, which is not of much use against troops in the present-day trench. Our defence lay in leaning up close against the front wall of the trench, which caused most of the force of the shrapnel burst to go over our heads. One morning I was hugging the wall of the trench as close as I could stick, when a "coal box" burst near by. It tore down a long section of trench wall, killing a number of men. I saw the explosion and the next thing I knew I heard some one saying:

"Ah'll bet ye' Joe's snuffed it noo', puir lad."

I stuck my head up out of what seemed to me to be a ton or two of rock and dirt and yelled: "No; not this time!"

You should have seen their faces. Some looked frightened and others relieved. In a second they began to laugh. Two or three of them helped me to my feet, and then the laughing became more boisterous.

"It isn't so d funny as you think," I said, getting a little peeved.

They turned me round and one of them held up the front part of my kilt in such a way that I could see the whole rear of the garment had been torn off. Certain portions of my anatomy were as guiltless of clothes as when I was born. A splinter of the shell, about fourteen pounds in weight, had given me a close crop. Then I had to laugh too, though I was somewhat battered and sore, but that night it wasn't so funny. I was almost frozen while on sentry go, and the next day it was just as bad.

As I have already told you, the transports were scarce, and we had little to eat, and absolutely nothing in the way of new equipment. It was all we could do to get ammunition. After shivering all day, I determined to have some clothes. Right in front of our position, about twenty-five yards from the trench, lay a dead member of H company whose name was Jock Drummond. Under cover of darkness, I sneaked out, and was almost beside the body, when a flare rocket went up. All of No Man's Land was lit up like day and I had to lie among the dead as if I had been one of them. It almost turned my stomach, but I did not dare to move.

The Germans were searching the muddy ground and the least motion on my part would have brought a dozen or so bullets my way.

Presently the light from the flare bombs died away, and I wriggled closer to what had been Drummond. I got my arm under the shoulders of the body, and started to crawl back to the trench. Twice a rocket went up, and I had to lie still for minutes with my ghastly companion. The second time, a German must have seen us move. Three bullets spattered against the ground a few inches from me, and one struck Drummond. I suppose I was twelve or fifteen minutes crawling back to the trench. It seemed fifteen years an interminable time. I was not yet thoroughly hardened to war, and it went against my whole nature; but I had to have clothes. We took the kilt from Drummond's body, and I wore it for weeks. Drummond, at least, got a decent burial, and a letter we found in his pocket we mailed to his mother, to whom it was addressed; so perhaps the deed done with a selfish purpose bore some good fruits after all. I may add that the stench of the dead lingered with me for a good many days.

The night after I got Drummond's kilt, the Germans attacked us. We had erected barbed-wire entanglements in front of our position. We had empty jam and bully-beef tins, also empty shell cases from field guns, strung on the wire in such a way that the least touch would attract attention.

In this manner we were notified that the Germans were in the act of striking at us. Now they were coming hundreds of them. There was a thin edge of humanity first, like the sheeting of water which precedes a breaker up a gently sloping beach. Behind it came units more closely bunched, and, still farther back, was a mass of soldiery almost like a battalion on parade.

It was murder to fire into that wall of misty grey but the men who made it were bent on murdering us. I was firing as fast as I could. On my right was a lad of nineteen, who was one of the 3rd battalion militia of the Black Watch a detachment sent to replace our losses.

"Pray God they may not pass the wire," he half sobbed with every breath. He was afraid, but he would not run. Every man is afraid in his first battle. The recruit's face was drawn and white his lips a thin, pressed line but he fired calmly. He did not mind the bullets, but he had not yet the "spirit of the bayonet," and he dreaded that they should pass the wire.

The first of the thin line was at the entanglement. Most of them dropped before they touched a wire, but others cut a single strand before a bullet found its berth. They died; but they had succeeded in their mission. A thread of life cut to sever a strand of wire!

The wave had risen and was breaking over the entanglement. They were beginning to get through. Here and there a man lumbered up the gentle slope toward our trenches only to fall before he reached them. The mass of them was worming through the wire now.

A shrill whistle blew. From our trenches came a sound like the beating of a hundred pneumatic hammers. It was the music of Hell. The machine guns and artillery were making it, and they were spitting out death in streams to the accompaniment of their devilish music. God was answering the prayer of the little lad. The Germans were dropping at the wire; they would not pass.

The wee death engines were playing just a foot or so above the bottom of the wire, and they were literally cutting the legs from under the mass of grey-clad men. The back wash from the wave which broke against the wire was thinner than the wash that had preceded it.

"Thank God!" gasped the boy; "I did not have to use my bayonet."

"It's guid steel wasted," growled a ginger whiskered old-timer on my left, as he wiped the dampness from the blade with his sleeve and dropped the bayonet back into its scabbard.

Today such an attack on the British lines would invariably be followed by a counter attack to show the Germans that the initiative lies—always must lie—with the Allies; but, in those days, we had not the men. Our lines were often so thin that, had they been pierced at a single point, we would have been crumpled up like paper.

After this fight, we were relieved by an East Yorkshire regiment and told that we would go to billets about three miles in the rear, but we had scarcely left the trenches when we received orders to get to billets and hold ourselves in readiness to occupy a new position in the line.

71

The Black Watch at that time was again brought up to strength by the addition of a reinforcement of five hundred men.

A party of us was sent to guard a bridge that our engineers were repairing, it having been blown up the previous day by big shell fire. I had just got off duty and was sitting before the log fire in the block-house with a few other fellows, when in popped a little Algerian, as black as the ace of spades. On recognizing that we were Scots, he held out his hand and said:

"My name's MacPherson; what's yours?"

He made himself right at home, and we shared our bully beef and biscuit with him. We had just been warming it. Our black "Scotsman" insisted on staying with us, and so we adopted him as a sort of mascot.

Shortly after we took up our new position in the line, a German sniper began to annoy us, and continued to do so almost ceaselessly. Every time anything showed so much as an inch above the crest, it drew fire, and a number of our men were shot passing traverses. There was a wood near our position, and we were pretty sure the fire was coming from there although we could not locate it. The Algerian was a crack shot, and wanted to prove it, so he went to our lieutenant and said:

"Me get sniper, if you like."

"Go ahead," said the lieutenant, half jokingly.

It seemed ridiculous to think of "MacPherson" with his tiny body and his face of a black angel "getting" anybody.

The little Algerian disappeared. At the end of three hours, after we had all given him up as lost or strayed, he returned, clutching a small untidy package rolled in a French newspaper.

"Well, then, he didn't eat you up, did he?" someone asked.

The little Algerian understood English poorly, but he

generally got the gist of things. This time he evidently thought he had been asked whether he had eaten up the sniper.

"Ugh!" he exclaimed; "me no eat sniper, but git him. Look here."

Very gingerly he unrolled his sheet of newspaper and, as evidence that he had landed his man, exposed to view a human ear. He wanted to present the ear to the lieutenant, but the officer declined the honour.

There was much night-patrol work to do on the Aisne. Often we ran into German reconnaissance patrols. One night I was scouting with another man. Five or six hundred yards from our lines, we came upon a boche sentry. He was a big, heavy fellow, and I remember thinking that he looked as if the hard army life had not yet worked the surfeit of beer out of his system. He was leaning on the parapet, and appeared to be asleep. We wanted to get beyond, as he was on the German advance listening post, but, as a reconnaissance patrol must conceal from the enemy all evidence of its proximity, we dared not shoot him. So we crawled to one side of him, and my partner, who was slightly ahead, gave him a thud on the side of the neck, which only, as we thought, made him sleep the more soundly. He dropped into the trench. The next moment a head bobbed up and the dose was repeated with the result that the boche (whom we had mistaken for the first man) slid back again. We looked over to see whether the second blow had done its work; there were two forms instead of one. My partner took a helmet as a souvenir. He kept it for one day and then abandoned it as inconvenient to carry. He found that a souvenir the size of a boche's helmet could not be put between the leaves of his *St. John's Gospel*.

Being about the only Black Watch scout left of those that had first landed in France, I had been almost constantly on duty during the fighting at the Aisne. You can imagine then how happy I was when we were relieved from the trenches and billeted a short distance in the rear in hay lofts, cottages, and stables.

On our way to billets we were looking forward to a "cushy" time, a good rest, a decent meal, and a wash, and hoping that the next section of trench we took over would be much quieter. It did not seem, however, as if I had had much more than the proverbial "forty winks" when we were sent back to support the Cameron Highlanders.

It was the Camerons who had just relieved us and their headquarters were in a quarry where ours had been. A few "coal boxes" had landed in the quarry, and reduced it to a mass of debris. Only one officer and bugler had survived. It was here that Sergeant Major Burt, of my native town, was killed. He was reputed to have the "best word of command" in the British army. We reached the scene in time to help the Scots Guards dig out some of them. It was a gruesome job. Some of the men had been pinned under heavy rocks for hours without losing consciousness.

There was, in particular, one instance of an officer— I cannot recall his name—whose legs were crushed and pinned down. His head had been cut by a shell splinter. When we tried to dig him out, he ordered us to attend first to a private, a few feet away, whose ribs had been smashed in and who was bleeding from the nose and mouth.

In all, about thirty officers and men lost their lives here.

We were called from this scene of carnage to defend a trench line against the Prussian Guards who were threatening to break through. The machine-gun and shrapnel fire was terrific, and for a time we were glad to squeeze ourselves close against the parapet. Then suddenly everything seemed uncomfortably quiet. Wounded were screaming and groaning all about us; men, who had not been struck, were muttering to themselves driven half mad by the bombardment; but, the instant the roar of the guns and shell explosions ceased, all seemed still. The Prussians were undoubtedly preparing to charge us, but they must have been slow in getting started. We got hurried orders to get ready to go over the top and surprise them.

I thought of but one thing as I ran forward; that was "Blighty."

On going to billets it had been my intention to write to the folks at home the next day after getting a rest, but our stay had been so short that to do so had been impossible. And now my thought was: "Perhaps I sha'n't return."

The Prussians seemed surprised by our quick attack, and the offensive was wrested from them. We became the assaulters. How I got through the entanglement I cannot tell. All I know is that I left part of my kilt dangling amid the wires. However, before we reached their trench line, the Prussians had scrambled over their parapet to meet us. In the general mix-up I found myself locked in the arms of a bear-like Prussian Guardsman who evidently had lost his rifle and bayonet. His knee was at my knee his chest pressed against my chest. Our faces touched.

I slid my hands up along the barrel of my rifle until they were almost under the hilt of the bayonet. Very slowly I shoved the butt back of me and to the side. Lower and lower I dropped it. The keen blade was between us. All the Hun seemed to know about wrestling was to hug. He dared not let go. Had he known a few tricks of the game, I should not be writing this today.

Instinctively I felt that the point of my bayonet was in line with his throat. With every ounce of strength in my body, I wrenched my shoulders upward and straightened my knees. The action broke his hold, and my bayonet was driven into his greasy throat. His arms relaxed; I was drenched with blood, but it was not my own. I staggered away from him, wrenching my rifle free as he fell.

The thrust I had used has come to be known as the "jab point"; they are teaching it to the American army to-day. It developed naturally from just such situations as I have described.

It was an awful melee. There were men swinging rifles overhead; others, kicking, punching, and tearing at their adversaries; while others again, wrestling, had fallen to the ground, struggling one to master the other. One Highlander, who had been struck by a bullet just before reaching the enemy parapet, grasped his rifle, and crawled as best he could the intervening distance, waiting his chance to get his man. At last it came. His bayonet found its mark, before the bulky Hun could ward off the unexpected stroke from the wounded lad. In a moment they were both lying prone on the earth. The Highlander, I am sure, died content that he had got his quota at least.

It was the wildest confusion, but its impressions were absolutely photographic. I can see it all, again, this moment.

The Prussians were finally obliged to retire to their reserve trenches. We took their firing trench, but had to vacate it because it was subject to an enfilading fire from the enemy. As we retreated in company squads, we kept up a steady fire.

While making for our trenches, I shouted to one of the fellows on my left to keep down as we were drawing the enemy's fire. The sentence was hardly completed, when something hot struck me on the left jaw. It seemed as if I had been hit with a sledge hammer. I spun round, stumbled, and fell to the ground. I realized that it was a bullet and tried to swear at the boches, but all I could do was to spit and cough, for the blood was almost choking me. The bullet, entering my cheek and shattering some of my teeth in passing, made its exit by way of my mouth. My warning, however, had saved the life of the lad I had shouted to. He flopped to the ground just in time to avoid a sweep of machine-gun fire, and managed to crawl to our trench, which was a very short distance off.

I was sent to the regimental dressing station. There were scores there more seriously wounded than I, and they were, of course, attended to first. By the time it was my turn, my face was so completely smeared with congealed blood that the orderly couldn't locate the wound. He wiped my face with a bunch of grass and applied a dressing. I was relieved to hear that it was a clean wound.

In the dressing station, suffering as I was, I noticed two men forcibly controlling a wounded comrade. After a moment I recognized him as the little recruit who had prayed that the Germans might not pass the wire and come to bayonet fighting with us. His features were so changed that he seemed aged a dozen years and believe it or not, as you will his hair, which had been sleek and black, was entirely white. He had been only slightly wounded but the heavy bombardment had driven him entirely mad. He was continually crying for his mother. I afterward learned that he and his mother, who was blind, had lived together and had been warmly devoted to each other, but at the outbreak of the war, his mother felt it her duty to send him to fight. The boy recovered his mental faculties a month or two after being sent home.

## CHAPTER 8

# Towards Ypres

After the first dressing of my wound, I was sent to our transport station, a short distance behind the lines, being told that in a few days I would be fit for duty again. There was a farm here. By the time I reached the farm house the pain of my wound was terrific. It was like a toothache all over my head and down into my neck and shoulders. Nevertheless, I threw myself onto a pile of straw in the barn and, after tossing about a while, managed to fall asleep.

When I awoke it was daylight again, the entire night having passed. Leaning over me was a little French girl she must have been about eight years old with a pitcher of milk, which she held out toward me. In spite of the condition of my mouth, I managed to swallow the milk. I was almost starved and very weak. I tried to persuade the little girl to accept a franc for the milk, but she shook her head, and skipped off. Following her out of the barn, I met her mother to whom, also, I offered payment; she, too, refused it.

We could hear the rumbling of big guns; shells were exploding not far away; then came the noise of transport wagons approaching the farm. I turned back toward the barn and had not gone more than ten paces when there was a crash overhead. Splinters and shrapnel spattered into the farm yard. I ducked and hastened my pace. Then there was a thud behind me, as if a bag of potatoes had been dropped from a lorry. Almost simultaneously came a scream from the little girl.

I turned just in time to see the mother of the child fall, roll down out of the doorway in which the two were standing, and lie ominously still. The little girl stood gazing in terror at the fallen woman. Her little hands were raised shoulder high before her and she shrieked hysterically and helplessly. As I hastened toward them the child seemed to realize the awful thing that had happened and threw herself upon her mother's body, pressing her face against the dying woman's.

I felt the tears trickling down my cheek and smarting in my wound as I heard the child's heartbroken exclamations terms of endearment they seemed, and pitifully eloquent enough, though the tongue in which they were spoken was unknown to me.

A lad of ten, barefoot and in overalls, came running from the house. He knelt and stared into his mother's face, then he turned a dumb, questioning glance at me. I could not meet his eyes. As I got my arms under the shoulders of the fallen woman and started to drag her body into the house, I could hear the little fellow sobbing softly but he didn't speak. Hoping that it still might be of use, he helped with all his little strength to move his mother's body. Inside the house, we pushed the tumbled hair back from her face. A shrapnel bullet had entered her forehead. It was useless to ask if human aid could serve her. Death had been almost instantaneous. Then I saw a sight that spoke a volume on the cruelty of war and the heroism of the sturdy French blood could I but tell it.

The little lad gathered his sister in his protecting arms and sat speaking, manfully, words of comfort to her beside the dead body of their mother, shells meanwhile bursting all about the home which had been their childhood haven of love and safety, and brick and plaster falling about them from its shattered roof. The children were in serious danger, but they steadfastly refused to leave their mother. I did not know enough French to reason with them, and it was not until some French muleteers sought shelter behind the building that I was able, through them, to persuade the boy and girl to go farther to the rear, with them.

After this experience, like one in a dream, I made my way back to the trenches, heedless of the shells whizzing overhead. The sight I had seen haunted me.

Upon reaching my trench, I was brought back to my senses by some of my "muckin' in" pals, who threw all sorts of questions at me in a jesting fashion, such as:

"Hello, Reuter, been tae Blighty an' back? Ye're a better sprinter than Ah thocht."

"Hoo's aw wi' th' fokes at hame? Did ye remember the fags?"

It was some time before I was sufficiently myself again to be able to answer them in the proper strain. My head looked like a cotton-and-bandage demonstration, and I was a sorry looking sight altogether. I lived for the next few days on bully beef biscuits, softened, and Oxo cubes dissolved in water.

In a few days we were relieved by French troops, and we force-marched north to stem the German thrust at Calais.

After some stiff marching, we entrained "somewhere." Our "camions" were coal trucks, which had been only partially unloaded. Some of my more hygienic mates who were under the impression that they did not have as much grime-caked mud sticking to them as the rest, suggested that our truck be cleaned out, but the general eagerness for a corner "doss" put this suggestion out of consideration at once. There was a scrambling match, and when our allotment got entirely in, the quartermaster was soundly "cussed." It seemed as if the whole regiment had been detailed to this car. Even in these circumstances, the whimsical philosophy of the private soldier asserted itself. A little chap, jammed in a corner, said he wanted a place by the side door, so that he could "see the scenery"!

We travelled all night, and on the following morning drew up at a junction where a body of recruits joined us. They regarded us with staring eyes, and I suppose we did look like a lot of cave men, being unshaven, longhaired, grimy, and black as sweeps with the coal dust. We did not mind this half so much as the recruits. At the junction, we got a sandwich and a canteen of coffee which had a most exquisite flavour of rum. This was so pronounced that some summoned their nerve sufficiently to go back for a "double attack," but were met with "Napoo."

Conditions have changed now, so that Tommy is able to keep himself shaved and personally neat, even in the mud of the trenches. It helps keep up our morale and shatter that of the boches. There is a distinct psychological effect on the enemy when clean-shaven, tidily-dressed men come up out of the earth and fall upon them.

Very soon we commenced our journey again. How long we were on the train I cannot recall, but finally we reached a large town where we got off. On our arrival we could hear the incessant rumbling of guns, and knew we were going to have another hot time of it. My face was better, but my beard! I had not had a shave since before Mons! While on the retreat, most of us, in order to lighten our loads, had thrown away the little items of our equipment that we did not urgently need. We kept only our greatcoats and such articles as we required for warmth.

We force-marched until early morning, when we halted for a rest, as the feet of many of our men were skinned and in bad shape. For myself, I was walking on my uppers, as the soles and heels of my shoes were completely worn out.

We resumed the march. We understood that we were in the vicinity of Ypres. We force-marched for all we were worth, and late in the afternoon we came to a village. Here we were billeted on the side nearest us. After getting rations, we needed no coaxing to sleep.

It was still dark when we got orders to fall in and march at top speed. The village was being shelled.

This seemed to have been a spot for concentrating for we met with other regiments there one of them the King's Royal Rifles. Beyond the far side of the village at a certain distance one could see trees scattered here and there, but farther on the country was flat. It was in this direction we marched.

Orders were whispered along the line that we were to maintain strict silence and no "fags" were to be lighted, as we were near the enemy, and were attempting to move without his knowledge. Our officers gave us the encouraging news that we were about to be up against some hard fighting harder than we had so far experienced. Our commander, Major J. T. C. Murray, expressed the hope that we would keep the name of the "Black Watch" where our predecessors had placed it in the foremost rank. And so we advanced in darkness, with our minds on serious things.

We were in two lines of skirmishing order, one pace apart. Our object was to reach the flat ground beyond the trees and dig ourselves in before dawn. We did this. The digging was an easy matter as the earth was marshy and our entrenching tools proved fit enough for the task. Shells were flying overhead continually, making an awful humming noise, and some of them passed so low that the air disturbances blew caps from off the heads of our men.

There was not a murmur or a word of complaint from

our wearied and worn ranks. We had almost completed our shallow trenches when the boche opened fire at us with his field guns. It was hardly dawn. We kept on digging, crouching in all positions to keep under cover from the bombardment.

I suppose that every one under shell fire, at one time or another, in some manner, prays. I know that I often have done so, although not so ostentatiously as some of the men. I have seen them, when the shells were rocking the earth and splinters were whistling past our ears, drop to their knees and swear to their Maker that, if they were spared, when they returned home they would go to church regularly and be kinder to their wives and children.

Some of our men ceased digging after reaching what they thought a safe depth, and crouched against the parapet for safety. Others of us started making what are known to-day as dug-outs. Jock Hunter and I made one to hold both of us. We dug away under the parapet so that we could crawl in with only our feet sticking out. This not only sheltered us from the unceasing shrapnel, but from the rain also. Some of the boys lying in the trenches had been killed and some wounded from the shrapnel bursting overhead, so the officers gave orders that we were all to make these dug-outs.

A man from each company had been detailed for look-out duty, at which we all took turn of an hour each. It was noon before we heard any response from our artillery, but then it checked the German fire considerably.

The rain came down heavily, flooding us out of our dug-outs, and we were obliged to stand in the trench like a lot of half-drowned rats, our greatcoats on and our waterproof sheets over them. At first we were standing on earth, but before long the muck had reached over our ankles.

There was at least one virtue in the rain it softened our

bully-beef biscuits, which we ate standing in the trenches, wet to the skin and with water dripping from our great-coats and kilts.

Toward night the rain ceased. We had expected to be attacked at any minute that day, but for some reason or another we escaped it. We got a rum issue. Then volunteers were asked for, to go and fetch some hot "gunfire." (It was hot when the ration party got it, but quite cold when it reached us.)

That night I was given orders to go on night reconnaissance. While I was away on this duty, the engineers came up and our fellows dug in again in advance of the old trenches. The engineers then constructed a barbed-wire entanglement in front of our position.

Wet and cold, and covered with mud, I went off on patrol duty, and many a shell hole I stumbled into to make me wetter. The enemy's position was about seven hundred yards from ours.

When moving between the lines, I noticed the outline of a big man. I don't know why I didn't fall down upon seeing him. My instinct told me to go ahead to make sure who it was. We were making straight for each other; as we met we almost brushed sleeves; then, with no more than a glance at each other, we passed on; but you may be sure that I had my jack-knife in the proper hand. I could not say even now whether or not he was a German.

I returned to our lines and, after reporting, helped to finish the trenches. I heard the following morning that one of our patrols had captured a German. I wondered if he might be the big fellow I had passed in the dark.

We received the order to "stand to" at dawn. Other troops had dug themselves in some distance behind us during the night. We got another rum issue just before "stand to"; it was highly appreciated.

At dawn, the Germans attacked in mass formation, but our rifle and artillery fire made big gaps as they advanced. They did not reach our trenches. They retired, leaving piles of dead. The nearest of their dead were not more than one hundred yards from us.

This time we had very few casualties in our battalion largely on account of our having dug in ahead of our old position, the range of which the enemy had. Their fire constantly over-reached us.

After this attack was over, we heard the buzzing of airplanes, and although we had been instructed not to look up the white of faces being very conspicuous from above we ventured to do so, and saw a British plane smash headlong into a boche machine. Both went end over end to earth, and the pilots undoubtedly were killed. The Englishman, in giving his life, had saved perhaps hundreds of us in the trenches.

In the afternoon, after a heavy bombardment, which tore up some of our barbed wire, the enemy made another charge. This time they came over in wave formation. The order was passed along to "fix bayonets," and, as soon as the Germans reached the barbed wire, to spring out and meet them. This we did.

We fought off line after line. The Black Watch suffered many casualties here, but not so many as the Germans. This crowd had less love for the bayonet than their brothers at the Aisne. Soon we were chasing them out beyond the barbed wire. We took many prisoners. If it had not been for the officer's whistle to retire, I think we would have driven them to Berlin, the way we felt that day. However, back we had to come.

The enemy's artillery fire began to pound on us as we were making for our trenches, and some of our fellows were bowled over as the result of it. As many of the wounded as we could bring, we brought back with us.

One fellow was lying about fifty yards away from the trench. Two of his mates volunteered to go out for him, but in the attempt they were wounded and forced to come back without him. Two others then went out; these managed to bring him in but he was dead. He was a young lad one of the latest to join our battalion. His equipment was practically new. I was given his shoes; they were much too big for me, but nevertheless I was grateful for them.

That night I helped to carry back more of the wounded, and, with the rest, assisted the engineers to fix up the barbed wire. This, coupled with the fighting of the day, well nigh exhausted me, but I didn't get the rest which I so much desired and expected, as I was detailed as one of our company ration party, comprising six men and a non-commissioned officer.

Owing to occasional shell fire, we were obliged to crawl close to the ground while on our way to the supply station. When we were coming back, the boches used flare lights which made us visible to them. I had a box of biscuits on my head. It made a fine target, and when I reached our trenches I found that bullets had pierced it.

# CHAPTER 9

# Scouting in Nomansland

For a day or two after this we had comparative quiet. Only bursts of shell fire threatened us, but these were so common as to be hardly noticed. The stench of the dead was terrible worse than we had yet experienced. Men turned sick and were positively useless for hours, many being sent to the base hospital for treatment for their violent nausea. Others developed rheumatic fever from sleeping in the mud and water.

Shortly after this, during the night time, we were relieved by an English regiment, composed of men who had not yet seen the worst of the fighting. They were fresh and inclined to be jovial. They asked rather carelessly about conditions as we had found them; we told them plainly what they had to expect. That seemed to sober them somewhat but not greatly. So we extended to them the conventional wish for the "best of luck" and left them to find out for themselves that they were in a campaign which could only be called one of present desperation and ultimate sacrifice.

Upon passing through an unidentified village, we found it deserted and nothing but a heap of ruins. The surrounding country as far as the eye could see resembled the lid of a pepper box, being full of shell holes. Many an oath came from the fellows, in the dark, as they stumbled into the shell holes full of water.

At last we reached our billets. Here, at least, there were signs of life. Troops and transports were passing us continuously, but we knew nevertheless that we were near the firing line, for we could hear the bursting of shells and see the flashes. The country was a little more hilly here, as far as we could see in the semi-darkness. We were more than glad to get into a stable or barn; it meant a chance to get dry and to stretch our overworked limbs.

After a little while we lined up in the farm yard and got some hot bully-beef stew in our canteens, a two-pound loaf among eight of us, some jam (needless to say "apple and plum"), and a "daud" of cheese; also a quarter-pound tin of Golden Flake cigarettes between two, and, as a sort of dessert, we got the mail from Blighty! Happy? why the word doesn't express it! We were simply elevated a million feet in the air tired as we were.

We discussed and played the different football league games over and over again as they were described in the newspapers we had just received. We imagined ourselves once more among the spectators at a cup-tie match between the Celtic and Dundee at Ibrox Park.

For a time war was entirely forgotten; but only for a time! With a sudden "jerk" we would be brought back to our senses and our present whereabouts by the voice of the orderly corporal asking whether Private McNeil, or Lance-Corporal Watson, or perhaps Corporal McGregor had been seen down the line wounded; or was he dead? It was war, all right, and not football we were playing at!

Jock Hunter and I were still "muckin'-in" pals, sharing our rations and troubles alike. Very soon the party broke, each man making for his allotted place to rest. I can recall so vividly the feeling that came over me as I lay down on that straw. It was identical with that which I had felt after coming back from a charge that had been a touch struggle! I fell asleep sighing and wondering how soon it would be when my letters would find no claimant for them!

We passed the next day writing letters, scraping the mud off our clothes, and at rifle inspection. More men joined us. One of the new arrivals lent me his razor, and I performed, what was, to me, the awful task of shaving. It made me feel like a new man, and they said I looked it. We were told that we would no doubt have a few days' rest, and then move to Dixmude or some town with a name like that. We were instructed not to leave our billets, and told that whenever we heard a boche plane overhead we should make for cover, or stand perfectly still with our backs to the walls of the farm houses, without stirring, until the machine was out of sight. That day we noticed a few of Fritz's sausage balloons in the direction of the firing line.

That night our officer, Lieutenant McRae, came round fully equipped; one look at him was enough; we knew there was to be no more "dossing" in the soft straw for us.

"Fall in at the double, men! We have to take over a new section of trenches not far from here." Such was the greeting he gave us. We got into "harness" all right, but how we grouched and cussed!

After lining up on the muddy road with the remainder of the battalion, the usual order was issued: "All fags out; no talking!"

We started off, wading through mud; with every now and then an occasional halt and more grouching in the ranks. With three hours of this to our credit, we found ourselves zigzagging round little hillocks along narrow muddy cart roads. We passed a concealed battery of small howitzers. Some of the English chaps noticed that we were "jocks" (the name the English give the kilties) and began cheering us up with:

"Down't wish y' enny 'arm but ye'r gowin' ta 'ave an 'ell of an 'ot tyme, you Jocks!"

We had ploughed our way through the mud only a few hundred yards beyond the battery when my nostrils sensed that there must have been some killing going on in the vicinity. A little farther on we came to an open section and turned to the right' just before making a small incline. I could see a few wrecked transport wagons and dead horses. We remained behind a hillock and were told that we were near the enemy. We were about to enter trenches which lay quite close to the German lines our officer told us, adding that we could have reached this point from our billets in half an hour, but that it was necessary for us to make the exceedingly long detour. Most of us knew that this was the direction in which we had seen the sausage balloon, which brought back the memory of the heavy firing.

We got into the natural ditches, which served us as trenches. We did not relieve any troops at this place, and there were no signs of any having been here, but on both flanks at some distance off, there were regiments entrenched. The situation was not one in the least to be desired. We were practically on an open space.

We were just in the act of starting work with our entrenching tools when all at once *"s-c-ch-eew!"* and the sky was alight with a flare rocket. There was no necessity for orders to hug the earth; we just simply flopped on our faces. Then it seemed as if the whole of the German artillery opened fire. We did not dare even to look up for quite some time. However, it seemed that we were not the party at which the firing had been concentrated; one by one our boys ventured to peep over in the direction of the flashes. The whizzing and groaning of the shells overhead was terrific, but they passed high. During the flashes, I looked over the open space in front of us. We were occupying a sort of high ground with slight mounds. To our right flank the country seemed more regular.

So far none of us had been struck, and we prepared to dig in properly. We had hardly levelled out our parapet, when an infernal noise of machine-gun and rifle fire let loose on our right flank some hundreds of yards off. Some of our look-out sentries seemingly got a bit nervous and commenced firing too at nothing. Then the whole line took it up. This racket kept up fully twenty minutes and we had not seen as much as a shadow. Shortly after this, Major Murray, our acting Commanding Officer, came along the line and gave orders to strengthen our position as the Germans were expected to make a big charge along the whole front in the morning. I was then told to select a man from my company (D) and go out between the lines to secure all the information possible with regard to the distance of the German lines from ours. Particularly, I was instructed to locate the places where they could crawl up in our direction without being seen.

There was no use asking for a volunteer for no sane person longed for this risky job, so I approached a strapping young fellow by the name of Lawson and accosted him with:

"Lawson, coming with me?"

"I'm with you," was his reply. Taking up his rifle, which had been leaning against the parapet, he added, as an afterthought: "But, whaur are ye bound fur?"

"We're bound for the German lines, to get information," I answered. I added that he had better hand over to a chum the keepsakes that he'd want his mother or his lass to receive as we might not come back again.

Dark as it was, I yet could see his chin fall and his face pale. With a very serious look and without another word he emptied his pockets. Very thoughtfully he took two packets of "Woodbine" cigarettes out of his haversack and handed them over to a chap sitting on the fire step with:

"Here, Donald, ye ken what tae dae wi' these if Ah'm not back afore mor-r-nin'."

We crawled out for about fifty yards, then, as there were little mounds in front of and behind us, we got up to our feet. We proceeded very cautiously, round the many little mounds, stumbling through shallow ditches, and crawling over the higher spots.

"Y' seem tae hae th' heng o' thees," said Lawson, as he stumbled and crawled behind me. "Ah'll dae mae best tae follow your lead. It's a braw new beesness tae me." He was referring to my method of keeping to natural cover.

"I've been trained in scouting," I replied. "Just do as I do, and with anything like luck we'll come out all whole."

Memory took me back to the days I had spent in scouting practice in India, under Major Bruce, the famous scoutmaster of the 2nd Battalion, Fifth Gurkhas; forty days, once, from Dunga-Gully up to the borders of Cashmere and back. Little did I think, in those days, that I'd ever find myself sneaking my way through the flats of Flanders, hiding from enemies in the air as well as on the earth.

Now and again we heard a rifle shot at times quite a distance away; then again, quite close. Often we'd hear the "swish" until at last, the bullet found its mark, with a "click."

We must have been out for over two hours, before we neared the German position. At last we could hear an occasional mumbling of hushed voices, and make out the dim outline of wire entanglements. The German position seemed to be on a little plateau.

While we were lying on our bellies, my partner could turn his face and look at me, but neither of us dared utter a word.

Fifteen minutes seemed like a century. I was more used to it than my partner, but even at that I must admit that I was as nervous as a man that is about to have a death sentence pronounced on him. It is the feeling that possesses every man that patrols "No Man's Land."

I motioned to Lawson, and we crawled away like worms that had been overlooked by a hungry crow. We reached our trenches quickly after getting into the broken ground; it was not until we had actually entered them that he opened his mouth. Then, approaching his friend, Donald, he demanded his fags. In a whisper, he triumphantly announced that we had been near enough to hear the Germans talking in their trenches.

I went to our officer and reported.

It was in the morning after "stand down," when our rum issue had been passed, that we learned what the racket had been the previous night. The Germans had tried a night attack on the King's Royal Rifles.

The morning was cold and misty. It was easy to see that we were about six hundred yards from Fritz's trenches, and that his, like ours, were on slightly higher ground than that which lay between the lines. There was a farm house here and there, behind us.

I could see a line of trenches on either flank but the one on the right was most easily perceptible. There was an open space at the end of our battalion line on the right flank, and our left flank was bent back slightly. We also learned that we had moved into this position without the Huns knowing that we were near. I could see the boche balloons some distance behind the enemy lines.

# CHAPTER 10

# Night Patrol

It was still morning when it was reported by one of our look-out men, who had been scanning the boche lines with a pair of field glasses (only his head showing above the top of the trench made for observation purposes), that the Germans were walking about the tops of their trenches in a careless fashion.

Naturally some of the last batch of men to join us wanted to have a pop at them, but our officers said no to let sleeping dogs lie. Most of us peeped over and saw them. Doing so, my eye caught a large number that had concentrated behind a mound to our right front directly in advance of the English troops that held a section of trenches on our right flank. I should judge that there were about a hundred of the enemy, some holding up white handkerchiefs in the lead, and a mass of them a little distance behind. My heart was in my throat, and I wondered whether the K. R. Rs were aware of their presence. I had heard stories of Germans with flags of truce. But so, evidently, had the commanders of the Rifles, for soon there was enacted before me a tragedy which I shall never forget.

About one hundred of the Rifles went forward to bring in this batch of Germans who were advancing apparently to surrender. They advanced very slowly and cautiously. Just when they were within short range, the Germans in front, bearing white flags but no arms, threw themselves onto the ground, machine guns began firing over their heads and those with rifles began firing point blank into the ranks of the British.

The K. R. Rs were ready for them. They opened up like a fan, their machine guns and rifles began crashing and the Huns were thrown into confusion. They dropped like clay pipes in a shooting gallery. The crews of the boche machine guns were picked off by the riflemen, and the K. R. R.'s machine guns kept on pouring lead into the mass. It was dreadful! I saw piles of Huns, dead and wounded, the latter waving like a shock of hay with some one underneath it trying to get out. Their officers, in the rear, shot down man after man who tried to run. They drove them forward like bullocks to the slaughter, for many of the Germans were too confused to shoot and scores had thrown away their rifles. Suddenly the K. R. Rs machine guns became silent. For a few seconds the rifle fire became faster and more furious. Then it stopped. Steel bayonets glinted as the K. R. Rs charged. There was no mercy shown. There were no prisoners taken. Of the five thousand Germans, who had gone out to do murder in cold blood, I do not believe five hundred got away. They were practically annihilated. The bayonets finished the work that the machine guns and rifles had started. What would you have? Men would not spare a nest of venomous snakes. It was a just retribution, but my stomach turned at it. None who had not seen it could even picture the sight.

For the next few days we had it "cushy," except for boche shrapnel showering our trenches at intervals, daily.

The cold, however, had increased enough to cause much discomfort. It was always cold, and especially so when there was a fierce wind and the rain drenched us. It was the common thing for the men to be up to their knees in water and slush.

We had been almost two weeks in this position when we noticed queer happenings in a farm house a few hundred yards behind our lines. The watchfulness of our officers revealed the significance of some apparently trifling things.

In the daytime, the shade on a window facing the German line would frequently be moved. Sometimes it would be drawn the full length of the window; then, if the German artillery had been pounding away at our right flank, immediately it would switch in the direction of our batteries. Sometimes the shade would be only half way down. More than once I saw a woman at this same window; and sometimes she would be leading a cow about some distance behind our lines. At night a light would be seen now and again moving past the window.

Agents of the British Intelligence Department, summoned to the front by our officers, discovered that a complete system of signalling was carried on between the people in the isolated farm house and the Germans. Three men and a woman were marched out of the house and taken away. After that, our concealed batteries, in new positions, hadn't a single casualty for days, whereas, previously, they had been almost constantly under heavy and accurate fire!

During the few days following the "white flag" affair, when the bodies' shelling was not quite so steady, we passed our time playing cards. Occasionally one of the fellows, who had split a piece of wood at one end, would insert a card in it and hold it over the parapet. Nine times out of ten a German sniper there were many of them in the vicinity would put a hole in it with a bullet.

These snipers caused us a great deal of trouble, particularly when we wanted water, which was procurable only at a little brook on our left flank. To get it was such a risky proposition that there were no "detail parties" formed in the daytime, and any one who went in quest of it, did so at his own risk.

Many a one who did so venture paid for his daring with his life. The snipers were always busy, even at night, and seemed to have a line on this spot.

A few of the fellows, rather than risk going to the brook, filled their water bottles from a duck pond full of a dirty, green, slimy liquid situated behind our line. The result was sickness to most of those that drank it and nearly all had to be sent to hospital.

Late one afternoon our section (thirteen men) was all together. Four of us were playing cards in an effort at distraction, for we were nearly insane from the lack of drinking water. For two days we had had to eat our bully beef and biscuits dry. We made it up that we should play a game of "phat" (a common card game among the Tommies), and that the one with the lowest count would have to take the section's water bottles and fill them at the brook. This to use a Yankee expression was a "cinch" for me, or at least I thought so at the beginning of the game; and so did the others, who, because of my record as a winner at the game were of the opinion that I couldn't lose.

However, toward the middle of the game I became nervous. So far I had taken only two tricks. Things got worse as the playing progressed, and it wound up with me the loser.

Without a word, they collected the thirteen bottles and hung them on my left shoulder like decorations on a Christmas tree.

Silently I made off. I reached the brook without mishap.

I had almost half of the bottles filled when zip a bullet struck very close to me. I tumbled into the water, pulling the bottles with me, and, in a lying position, continued filling them. This was not what one might call a comfortable or a convenient position in which to fill water bottles. They filled very slowly indeed.

As soon as they were full, I placed them on my shoulders; rose, dripping, from the water; and made for our line. I had not gone more than twenty paces when a bullet struck close at my heels. I jumped and looked upward, hoping to fool the sniper into thinking he was firing too high, causing him to set his sight for a shorter range. The next shot fell shorter still. I looked up again and hastened my pace. A third shot visibly struck a rock and enabled the sniper to correct his range.

Almost immediately after came another bullet, which I knew had got something about me. Instantly I flopped down and lay still. There was more scattered firing from the German lines and I was trembling with "nerves."

At last, I could not stand it longer. I was afraid the sniper would fire at me again not an uncommon practice with the boche sniper, who, when he drops his man, usually sends over a make-sure shot. So I sprang to my feet and rushed for the trenches, arriving there in safety.

When I got into our section I found my pals sitting around and looking very gloomy. Upon seeing me they greeted me with:

"Ye've been a h o' a time awa'. We were juist beginnin' tae think we'd lost our watter bottles."

When I unloaded my cargo I found that two of the bottles had been pierced by a bullet. Each man of the section made a thirsty effort to lay hands on his own bottle. I was left with the two damaged ones besides my own.

Then they told me how a shell had exploded and killed two of the card players the owners of the damaged bottles. The water that was left in these was distributed among the others.

Patrol work, mostly at night, continued to be my chief duty. On one occasion I lost my bearings, and presently found myself almost upon one of the boche listening posts.

"So long as I have come thus far, I will edge in and take a chance," I said to myself.

I knew it would be almost as dangerous to go back as to go forward, for at any moment a man might crane his neck above the parapet, see me moving, and fire. Then there was the momentary chance that a star bomb would light the heavens and all the earth between the lines, in which case a thousand rifles would begin sputtering at everything that moved or seemed to be alive. Each second I expected it to come. My nerves felt as if they were drawn taut taut as the barbed wire which the boches string so tight that if it is cut in the night it will twang like the string of a violin. But the quick shot in the night did not come, and I wriggled forward through the wire.

I was almost at the edge of the parapet of the listening post. I heard voices whispering in German. Some one was scrambling up over the parapet. How was I to get away? I could not, so I lay on my belly and buried my face in the earth the earth which should be wholesome and life giving, but which stunk with unspeakable things.

Three heads appeared above the parapet. Shoulders followed, and cautiously a patrol of three men wriggled out from the listening post and then separated. One of them, in getting out, slipped, and I could hear him " strafing " under his breath, as he vanished into the night. Another head thrust itself above the parapet. I was sure a pair of eyes were staring at me, though I could not see them in the dark.

Once more I lay as if dead. "What's the difference?" I thought; in a few moments, probably, I would be, and then I should not mind the sight or the odour of what was around me.

The man in the listening post reached down for something at his feet. I was sure that he was going to hurl a grenade in my direction. Something came hurtling through the air. I sunk my teeth into my lip to keep from crying out, and wondered how the explosion would feel whether there was any anguish in being torn to bits instantaneously. The dark object plumped onto the ground at my side and bumped against my ribs. How long it took for it to explode! Then I knew it was only a stone. I continued to lie as still as one dead.

Another stone struck my shoulders. The sentry did not wish to rouse the whole line and start a wastage of ammunition by causing a thousand rounds or so to be fired uselessly into the night, as would probably be the case should he discharge his rifle or throw a grenade. He crawled up over the parapet and wriggled toward me. I tried to prepare myself to spring up when the time came, but I dared not so much as move a foot to get a better grip on the ground. He himself did not dare to rise. He knew that his silhouette would draw fire from the trenches. It would be like a battle between snakes, both of us on the ground there, fighting each other on our bellies.

I saw the dull gleam of his bayonet. Still I did not dare to let him know I was alive. He was only inches from me. I could hear his deep breathing. He was not sure whether or not I was a corpse, but he was going to take no chances. He lunged with the steel. I managed to jam the butt of my rifle against his head. It disconcerted him, but there was not enough force behind the blow, struck from my awkward position, to stun him. He rolled upon me. I felt for his throat. He was a big, greasy boche and my fingers could scarcely encircle his neck, but I squeezed and squeezed, for my life depended upon my eight fingers and my two thumbs. If I did not throttle him, he would kill me.

He was getting weaker. I felt his muscles relax. I could see his eyes. I do not think I shall ever forget them. They bulged from their sockets and it seemed that they would pop from his head and strike me in the face. It sickened me, but it was his life or mine. He was clawing frantically but weakly. Now he was still. It was brutal, but war is brutal.

After emptying his pockets I crawled to the edge of the dugout listening post. Inside were three men, two lying in the bottom of the hole, the third sitting with his back against the wall of the excavation. The boche I had just left probably had disobeyed orders in crawling out without awakening one of them. The error cost him his life and saved mine.

For a second as I peered over the edge of the hole I had thoughts of a daring deed, but it was better to get back to our lines with the contents of the first man's pockets, which no doubt afforded information for pur staff, and so I returned battered and torn and exhausted.

After this, in recognition of my work as a scout, I was offered the rank of a non-commissioned officer, but I did not wish it. They were picking off the non-coms too fast to suit me, and there was danger enough in the work I was doing.

# CHAPTER 11

# Snipers

After spending a few more days in this last, very warm position, we moved to billets a little way off behind our left flank, and we certainly needed the rest. There was no indication that these billets had been used before by our troops. Jock Hunter and I were assigned to a barn, and you may be sure I was delighted at the prospect of literally "hitting the hay" as the Americans say.

As there were chickens running around, even over every part of the thatched house, Jock and I went in search of eggs, for oh! how we longed for a change of diet! For weeks it had been bully beef and biscuits, and then biscuits and bully beef. In our search, we climbed up the ladder to the attic, which we found to be very spacious, with heaps of straw on the floor here and there. The walls of the structure, I should judge, were about four feet thick, and there was a space that wide where the parapet of the wall and thatching came near together.

On reaching the attic we could hear the voices of our fellows in the farm yard below. The noise came through the opening between the parapet and thatching which was supported by beams. The aperture must have been about a foot in height. Approaching this with the intention of playing a trick on the boys by throwing a piece of stone from the top of the wall I noticed, dangling over the edge, a black leather strap. Carelessly I gave it a sharp tug, when out came a "Colt," the handle of which I instantly caught. I scarcely had it in my hands when a man's head popped up and I found myself facing a German soldier. He started to reach to his side but I had him covered. I do not know whether he or I was the more greatly surprised.

"Hands up, ye swine!" I shouted, holding him cowed with his own revolver, although I was entirely ignorant of its mechanism, and did not even know how to release the safety catch.

He slid out of the recess under the thatch which he had been occupying and stood on the floor. With his hands up, he kept muttering:

"Mercy! *Kamerad! Kamerad!*"

Jock seemed stunned at this sudden and unthought of "find."

I asked him to tie the boche's hands, which he did with his rifle pull-through, and we marched him down to the officers' quarters. The officers were just preparing to eat, and were astounded at the sudden appearance of the boche in the doorway, as we made him walk in first. We left the prisoner and his Colt with the officers. Then we returned to search the loft.

In the deep recess over the wall we found a French rifle, a British rifle, several days' rations, ammunition, and a warm blanket which Jock and I snuggled under that night. It was a sniper's post and afforded an excellent view of part of our lines, especially the spot at the brook where so many of our boys "went West" in the act of getting water, and where I had had a narrow escape.

The next morning, after reveille, a corporal and three men who had done guard over the sniper got orders to take him to a given place, which was about three miles behind our lines. Also they were ordered to report back within "fifteen minutes from starting time."

We were promised a few days' rest here, but the following day, toward nightfall, we were shelled out of the place by the body's heavy artillery, the "coal boxes" landing all around the place. We had scarcely time to get out of it. Luckily enough, no one "clicked." We then moved to trenches near La Bassee. Here also was a great number of troops concentrating.

We had heard that our native troops from India were to hold part of the lines near us. Also we had been told of the great work the Canadians had done recently around this section, and we were looked upon to do the same. It was now December, and the sleet and rain poured on us for the first few days without cessation.

In the trenches here, in some parts we were knee deep in slush, and this had a very dispiriting effect. It, together with the continuous downpour of ram and sleet and Fritz's shelling which never ceased reduced us to a state of positive misery. We fared badly enough, but we wondered how the native troops (who were now on our left flank), used to a warm climate, could stand it.

We got more tinned rations and in greater variety, here, than I can remember ever having before. There was "Maconochie"-a soup with directions to boil fifteen minutes before opening the tin; which, of course, was merely satirical. The "Maconochie" was never warmed until it had reached our stomachs. However, it proved a very acceptable change from our "bully beef." That is, it did when it came. It didn't come often. We also had tins of muckin (butter) which Tommy says is a very good quality.

Another tinned product, but not a ration, reached us here. It was the famous jam-tin hand grenade which came into use at about that time.

Preparations were now in progress for an attack of greater magnitude than any we had yet taken part in. With a number of other scouts, I was sent out to examine the terrain over which our men would advance. The party was discovered by German snipers, and we ran back to our lines as fast as we could go. A piece of a ricochet shot struck my left ankle, but only slightly injured it on account of my heavy spats and leather shoes, so that by having a tight bandage applied at once I was able to take part in the attack.

Hitherto most of our engagements had been more or less surprise affairs that is, we would get word of the enemy just about in time to be ready for him when the actual charge came. This time it was different. We had been told what time we would go over at them. We had to sit around and wait. Some of the men were carefully cleaning their rifles. Others ran their thumbs along the edges of their bayonets. Many were writing letters. But almost every face that I could see was pale. The greater part of them were nervously puffing away at fags, very often unlit.

Here and there a man would glance at his watch furtively, as if afraid it would be thought that he was hoping the time had not yet come. Others were swearing softly and grumbling because they could not charge at once.

Occasionally a man would joke or tell a funny story. Those who heard him either looked as if they hadn't heard or laughed rather thinly. It is one thing to go at them with steel and rifle, but quite another to sit around and wait for the short blast of the whistle which sends you out to kill or to be killed.

Our artillery was pouring shells and shrapnel upon the Huns and their guns were replying. The combat wagons with the ammunition and the wagons with the rations had to reach us through a curtain of fire. One hundred extra cartridges were distributed to every man, also extra tins of "bully." I was on my way to regimental headquarters with a message, when a shell squarely struck a transport wagon. It was obliterated. Men were torn into shreds. I saw the whole forequarters of a horse blown. high into a tree and caught there in a crotch. The stretcher bearers picked up some of the men. Some they could not even find. I was soon back again in the firing trench. We had gouged out little footholds to help us over the top.

At last it came the little shrill metallic blast we had been waiting for. It could be heard distinctly above the roar of the artillery. The blood surged back into the faces of the pale men. We were fighting now. It was different from the waiting and thinking the thinking of what we may be leaving behind us for always.

I was the first man out of the trench not that I was brave, but because I had already learned that it was the last man up and the last man down who usually are shot. I sped ahead of all the platoon; for in that lay safety.

It is a fact that men in trenches will fire at the mass in rear rather than stop to aim at a single runner out ahead. Each man seems to feel that he is sure to hit someone if he fires into the mass and that another will pick off the leader.

We were back again in our own trenches. What had happened in the charge I did not know. I can honestly state that my mind is a blank for the period of time which elapsed after I ran the first fifty yards toward the boches.

I was sitting on the fire-step. We had taken their trenches and had been recalled after our troops from the rear had gone forward to prepare the captured position against the counter attack which would surely come.

My chum, Jock Hunter, was sitting near me.

"Blow —— Coffee up," he said to me, laughing. I thought he had lost his senses. I stared at him blankly. "Blow —— Coffee up," he repeated, pointing to my side.

I glanced down at my hip. There was a battered bugle hanging from a cord over my shoulder. I was more bewildered than ever, but I unslung the instrument and we examined it. It was a bugle of the Potsdam Guards and there were thirteen bullet holes in it.

Jock would not believe that I did not know how I came by the thing, and you may find it difficult, too, to accept my statement, but it is a fact. I do not know how I got it. The period of the charge is a slice of my life which is completely gone from my memory. I do not know what sights I saw nor what sounds I heard.

On our first Sunday in this position, the German artillery became quiet about ten o'clock, and, about half an hour later, we heard strains of music from beyond the slightly risen ground on Fritz's lines. They were holding a Sunday service. But as soon as it was over, we were greeted with a couple of hundred shells from their artillery, so we came to the conclusion that the sermon must have been rotten.

The weather conditions here were so bad that a number of our fellows were sent to the base hospital with frost-bite, or what is known now as "trench feet." They suffered excruciating pain. I saw one fellow who had to have his shoe cut off; the foot swelled up instantly to very great size and was almost entirely black.

As a supposed protection against the conditions which had caused so many cases of "trench feet" some bureau expert over in England had a supply of rubber boots forwarded to us. I have seen many things which were useless supplied to soldiers but never anything to equal these boots. They were so loose and clumsy that they materially interfered with the action of walking and they were just of a height to be entirely submerged in the trench mud, leaving the wearer with an individual and separate bucketful of the stuff to lift with each foot. I heard many a pair wished on the Kaiser's feet. Big ladles with long handles also were distributed among us to be used in scraping out the water from the trenches, and each of us took our turn in acting as "chef," that is, ladling the water out behind the trench wall. Occasionally where a fellow, slow in throwing it over, would hold the ladle up a few seconds too long—*ping!* —a bullet would go through it. If we wanted to sit down the only thing we could do was to place our packs and equipment on the fire-step and sit on them.

Our position was somewhat lower than that of the Germans, as they occupied a sort of ridge. For days and nights at a time we did nothing but wait, with an occasional raiding party or artillery encounter, with now and again a heavy bombardment, to break the tedium.

We were sitting around in the mud one day when, all of a sudden, a heavy rifle and machine-gun fire swept along our trench. Then we heard a dull muffled roar as if some tremendous weight, padded heavily with bales of cotton, had fallen a great height. That is the only way I can describe the sound. Instantly, I wondered what had happened. I do not suppose it was a second later before I knew, but it seemed as if it were a full minute. The earth seemed to rock. There was a swashing, hissing noise. Mud, water, and stones poured down all around us. Muddy water cascaded into our trench. Clambering out of it and through a storm of bullets, we made for our reserve trench. Many of our men fell in the act of fleeing for shelter. This was the result of the Germans having dammed up their own trench which was filled with water, and dug tunnels in our direction as far as they possibly could without our being aware of it. They opened the dams just after commencing the firing. Their intention was to catch with the fire those that escaped drowning, and thus annihilate us, so that they could break through our lines at this point. No doubt it was a clever ruse, but it did not work.

## CHAPTER 12

# Bombing

Our regiment was now shifted from the position where the Germans had tried to drown us out to another section near a place which we afterwards christened "The Glory Hole." The German lines and ours were very near to each other here. On the night of our arrival we could hear the Huns talking, and after we had settled ourselves in our trenches, we could hear them now and again whistling *Highland Laddie*. It was evident that they knew who we were, as that is the tune to which we "march past." I was now initiated into the use of the hand grenades. The kind we got were later termed the "hairbrush."

Now and again, the Germans would take a mad turn and lob a few of their grenades over at us, and in turn, we returned the compliment. This form of fighting was then in its infancy, and we nearly all had our own ways of doing it. I used to tie two or three of the bomb handles together with a rope; get hold of the end of it, which was knotted; and, in the same way as an American athlete throws the hammer, I would swing the bombs over my head and let go in the direction of Fritz. In this way I could accomplish a few yards more than anyone who threw in the ordinary way.

Sandbags were piled about three feet high on top of the parapet with loopholes through which we fired our rifles.

When I wanted to throw the grenades in the fashion I have just described, I would go to the more level ground at the back, throw them, and jump back into the trench where I always had ample room, as the others, with varying criticisms of my enterprise, gladly cleared the way before I started operations. They fully expected me at some time to make a mistake and land the grenades among them instead of in the bodies' trench.

As we did not have one common system of throwing these grenades, a few of the noncoms and men were selected to practise a little way behind the lines the proper method. Our Acting-Colonel, J. T. C. Murray, and three men were killed when a lance-corporal, in swinging a grenade, accidentally struck the ground with it, causing it to explode.

At times we were treated to some lyddite shells by the boches (at least we believed them to be lyddite, though I have since learned that they were gas shells). I was never caught in the fumes myself, but I saw many men who had been. This particular gas simply snuffed the life out of the men without their even knowing what had happened. As they lost consciousness, they turned a yellow-brown colour, and never made any attempt to stir just went to sleep and did not awaken while those who got just a slight touch of it, would stagger about, as if deeply intoxicated.

Volunteers were asked, one day, to go to a V-shaped sector where the British and the German lines were so close that grenades could be easily thrown from one trench to another and they were! Thinking that it would be an easier job than what I had been doing, I gave in my name. I think nearly half of my company volunteered, but I was among the first eighteen to be picked. We were armed with grenades enough to do an hour's bombing. Two of the men were detailed to keep renewing the sandbags as they were torn down by the boches' constant bombing. The German grenades, set with a time fuse, exploded a few seconds after leaving the thrower's hand. The boches were evidently nervous about these grenades, for they almost invariably cut the time fuse too long or threw the bomb too soon after cutting it, so that our men frequently caught the unexploded grenades and hurled them back at the Germans.

The first two to go "west" when our volunteer party got into action were the sandbag men, and at the end of that hour there were only four of us left to come out of that Hell, ten being killed and four badly wounded. After our turn, volunteers were entirely out of the question, so each section had to take an hour at it. The trench point where the bombing occurred was called the "Glory Hole," and it was well named.

Upon getting back to the trench, I swore off "bombing," and decided that I would stick to scouting, although almost all the old scouts had been killed. Why I was not, is still a mystery to me. After a few days at the "Glory Hole" we were sent to the rear to billets.

You will remember that there were thirteen bullet holes in the Potsdam bugle which I brought back from the charge on the German trenches near La Bassee. How many of them were made after the bugle came into my possession and was put in my pack, I do not know, but, at any rate, I believe that thirteen is my lucky number. This is the reason:

After a short rest in billets, we were returned to a portion of the trench near a part we had occupied before. The regiment had been recruited up to full strength again, and I can tell you that there were very few of the original Black Watch left. In fact, the personnel that we now had was almost a third regiment. In order to reach the high broken ground to our right, where there was a great deal of patrolling and scouting to be done, it was necessary to cross an absolutely exposed strip of ground about thirty yards long.

So many men had been killed here that we called it "crossing the bar" when we had to traverse this neck of land. You must remember, we did not have a decent air fleet in those days and infantry patrolling and scouting were much more important than they are to-day. From the high ground to the right, much information of the movements of German troops could be gained. Whenever they saw even a single man "crossing the bar," the Huns would let loose a salvo of artillery fire.

I usually waited until it was dark enough to see the flashes of their guns before crossing this strip, and whenever I saw the first flash I would sprint a few paces toward it and then flop down. The Germans had the range exactly. By sprinting, I stood a good chance of getting in ahead of the burst, and as shrapnel carried forward, the ruse worked nicely. In order to show a party of the new scouts the way across the bar, I was sent out with twelve of them, thus making a party oj thirteen. Before we started I drew a rough sketch for them and told them, as exactly as I could, just what to do when we were fired upon. That we would be fired upon was a certainty.

About the centre of this open strip was the dried bed of a stream between deeply worn banks and this afforded the only protection on the way across. When the light was just right, we moved out to the edge of the bar. I gave my men a few last instructions. It was time to go. I took one last look across the ground which was literally covered with shell splinters and deeply furrowed.

"Rush!" I yelled. We went forward in a thin line.

I saw the expected flash of the guns.

"Straight toward them!" I shouted; and we all ran madly in the direction from which the shells were coming.

"Down!" I roared with every bit of voice that was in me, at the same time flopping down flat on my face.

There was a terrific crash! It seemed all around me. I could not tell whether it was in front or behind. I was surprised that I was not hurt. I heard groaning behind me. One of my men was wounded. There was not another sound. I thought the others must have kept on running despite my instructions, and were now in the little bed of the stream waiting for me. I dared not move. I had to lie as one dead or the guns would have begun crashing again and they would get me and the wounded man behind me. Flare rockets illumined the sky. I prayed that the man who was hurt would lie still. If he hadn't done so it would have been all over with both of us.

Half an hour I lay there in the mud until the rockets were no longer going up and I thought it safe to move. I crept a few feet over the ground. My hands were upon the body of a man, but he was not groaning. Yet the groaning continued from nearby. I realized that one of my men had been killed. I crept farther in the direction of the groaning. I bumped into a huddled mass. It was another body.

Still I groped around. I had found three now. At last I reached the man who was hurt. He wasn't moving, only groaning. I thought that there were others of the little party who needed help. In the darkness I wriggled here and there. I found another body. That made four. Then five six seven and so on till I found eleven. There were only two of us left the wounded man and myself!

I stood up despairing and like one lost. I almost wished that I had been one of the eleven who had "crossed the bar" once for all. I got the wounded man onto my shoulder in the style which is known as "the fireman's carry," and started back with him, walking erect. I had forgotten the danger of shells. Luckily it was inky dark and I was not seen.

I staggered against a part of our barbed wire entanglements. I called for help. Four men crawled over the parapet

113

to meet me. They dragged the wounded man to the edge of the parapet. He was still groaning faintly though he lay as one dead. As we lifted him over the edge of the trench, the groaning ceased. He was dead! *I* alone of the thirteen had come back alive!

While we were laying out the corpse, we heard the look-out sentry halting some one. I jumped onto the fire-step and plainly saw a figure straightening up on our side of the barbed wire, with his hands over his head, coming right forward. He dropped into our trench, of course with the sentry holding his bayonet pointed at him. It was plain to be seen that the young German was giving himself up, no doubt being sick of the fighting. He made a motion as if to put his hand inside his coat, but the man with the bayonet was taking no chances and made a lunge at him, which greatly frightened the lad. So he made us understand as well as he might, still holding his hands aloft, that he had something in his pocket he wanted to show us. The sergeant stepped over and took out the contents of the pocket. He did not have any firearms at all. Among the few things in his pocket was a worn plain envelope, and at this he pointed. Inside was a sheet of paper and on it was written in good English:

"English soldiers, please be kind to my boy."

The sergeant asked me to take the boy back to the officers' quarters with him, as I had yet to report my sad experience in "Crossing the Bar." The case of the boy prisoner proved an extraordinary one. An officer of the engineers attached to the Black Watch, who could speak German, questioned him. The boy had not the least idea what the fighting was about. He told the officer that his mother had given him the letter as she felt sure that the English would be kind to him. She had told him that he should give himself up at the first opportunity. He was her only son.

We learned from him of preparations for an attack by the Germans at dawn, which corroborated the information our staff already had. He was treated very kindly. He seemed very much taken aback at the kind treatment accorded him, and asked if it was the custom of the English to treat prisoners kindly before torturing and putting them to death. Upon hearing this, the officer he was speaking to laughed uproariously for fully a minute, and the others wanted to know the joke. He told them and some joined in the laugh. The officer patted the boy on the back; gave him his letter, telling him at the same time to treasure it; and said that he would no doubt meet his mother again.

The boy fell upon his knees and tried to kiss the officer's hand, sobbing like a child. But the officer nearly turned a backward somersault, getting away from the hand kissing, and swore as if he would eat the lad up.

Sure enough, the next morning the attack came off, but we were prepared for it. Just at "stand to" before dawn, our artillery opened fire and kept pounding at them until about eight o'clock; the enemy replying very vigorously. They attempted to get over their parapet, but gave it up until about noon. They tried it again. Our artillery opened up on them, and some forces along our line charged the Germans.

The Black Watch had supports up and were to make a charge at two o'clock that day, but the sleet came on with an awful wind, and this prevented it. Instead, the regiment in support came up and took our place in the trenches. We moved along some distance to the right flank. The sleet and rain continued, also the wind. We were cold, miserable, and grousing in good style because we found we had to take another part of the trench, instead of going, as we thought, to billets. However, we got an extra issue of rum.

This place was pitted with big shell holes.

It looked extremely weird. One *sigarree* (fire box with charcoal) was issued to a company, and we would take our turn in getting warmed up from it. This lasted only a few days, for very soon the Germans sighted the smoke, which drew their shell fire, and so we were glad to abandon the *sigarrees* and suffer the cold.

## CHAPTER THIRTEEN

# The Dark Curtain

We were by no means well acquainted with our new position, and one night shortly after our arrival, two of the men who had been sent out to reconnoitre, were captured by the enemy, who let them go, however, after stripping them to the skin.

When they returned they had big bayonet wounds in their hips, and were suffering greatly both from the wounds and exposure. You can imagine our feelings at such wanton cruelty.

Previous to this for some time I hadn't been given any scouting duty and had been resting, but a few nights after this occurrence, shortly after dusk, I was sent to a listening post, which was situated to the right front of our open flank. The ground was very broken and the temperature was touching on the zero mark. Before starting out, we had just got our night issue of rum. A lance-corporal accompanied me, and after lots of manoeuvring and stumbling through shell holes half filled with slush, we arrived at the place where I had to listen for movements of German artillery, transports, troops, etc.

We crawled to the edge of the bank, which overlooked a creek or canal. We knew the German lines were just across that short space. The lance-corporal said he would see that some one should be sent to relieve me in half an hour; then he departed. He had not gone more than a hundred paces, I should judge, when the German artillery let loose. It seemed as if a thousand hells had erupted. I was dumbfounded. I wiggled backward on my stomach, until I slid into a shell hole full of water and mud. I did not mind the cold; it helped to brace me to realize fully the situation in which I was placed. The shell fire was lighting up the heavens; splinters, slugs, and bullets filled the air.

I began saying my prayers. (I thought this would be my last listening duty on earth.) I crouched as low as the slush in the hole would allow me. Even while in this position, bullets and shrapnel embedded themselves so near me that, had I lifted my head, I should have been plugged instantly.

The hellish bombardment seemed unceasing. I was cramped and numb. How long the firing lasted I do not know. At last, however, I became conscious that the clouds were clearing away and I discerned a pale moon. I tried to drag myself out of the freezing slush, but couldn't. All the power in my body seemed gone. The shelling had ceased and there was a dead silence. I knew I was freezing to death. I once even tried to place the muzzle of my rifle under my chin and blow my head off, but I was unable to feel for the rifle. My hands had lost sense of touch. My lower limbs were insensible. I gave up all hopes of help or of ever leaving the shell hole alive.

What seemed a long time after I had deemed myself lost I heard some one in the vicinity. I wasn't able to lift my head. I tried to speak. I was as one dead, with the exception of my brain.

The next thing I knew something was being poured down my throat. Some one was attending to me but I was unconcerned. I wanted only to die. If I could but have spoken, I would have begged the men who were attending me to put me out of my agony. After a while, I recognized them as our men. They were rubbing and slapping my body for all they were worth. Now and again one of them put his water bottle to my mouth. At first I could not make out what he was trying to pour down my throat, but at last I recognized it as rum. I forced myself to drink it. Then they rubbed my abdomen and legs with some of it as briskly as they could. One of them exchanged his kilt for mine; then they both wrapped their greatcoats around me, and, between them, managed to carry me back to the trenches to safety.

The jolting on the way back started my blood circulating. It is beyond me to explain exactly the feeling. My stomach began aching as if it contained boiling lead; then a feeling as if a million electrically charged wires had commenced to burn in the lower part of my abdomen and down to my lower limbs. I had the desire to shout out loud; whether or not I did, to this day I cannot tell.

I must have gone completely insane with the pain for a while, for later I found myself struggling with a group of men, and they were urging me to keep quiet. They poured lots of rum into me, and I began to feel much better; in fact, more like myself, except that my legs and feet were like lumps of lead.

During this time since my rescue from the shell hole the Germans had made a charge and were repulsed. The Black Watch had taken a line of their trench and were holding it. Two men had been sent out to find what had happened to the lance-corporal and myself, as the company commander had been expecting our report. They found the lance-corporal, riddled with bullets, not far from where he had left me. When they came across me I had done an eight hours' stretch of duty.

I stayed in the reserve trench until we went to billets, a couple of days after this. We were looking forward to spending Christmas in billets, but were disappointed.

We had hardly been "cushy" three days, when we were sent to hold a position on the left flank of an English battalion of what we believed to be the Sussex Regiment. It was just two days before Christmas when we took up this position.

It was much quieter here. Snow had fallen during the night, giving the ground a sort of peaceful appearance, except for a few dark patches where some "Jack Johnsons" or "Black Marias" had landed toward dawn. (It was Christmas Day.) Just after "stand down," our mail was issued. It consisted mostly of parcels. Our part of the trench was very fortunate. Every man had at least two letters and as many parcels. I received three in the same handwriting and a two pound box of chocolate almonds. Parcels containing socks, mittens, scarves, etc., were pounced upon by all hands, as these articles were very much needed at this time. Next in importance came the cigarettes, of which we received a goodly supply.

I need hardly say that we all tasted one another's luxuries shortbread, chocolates, and currant cakes (which had to be eaten mostly with a spoon because of the rough handling they had had) and we exchanged confidences about our letters whether they were from Miss Campbell, Mrs. Low, or Uncle Sandy.

Every Tommy, every Jock, learns to know and to love his trench mate as a brother. The men in the "ditches" feel as if they all belonged to the one mother, sharing each other's confidences, both pleasant and sad. There is no selfishness not even a thought of it "over there."

We were all sitting round the fire-steps of our trenches, thinking, ever thinking, and wondering how many of us would live to see the same sun rise on another Christmas Day. The sun was red. It appeared to be dripping red with blood, when a slight commotion started up along to the right. I grasped my rifle and at the same time looked round the little traverse. I saw a few chaps with their heads over the parapet which seemed unwise and extremely danger-ous. I thought we had been surprised by the Huns, and took a glance in the direction of their trenches, which looked as quiet as our own. But I could see thin lines of smoke ris-ing up at irregular intervals from the fires they had built. Almost at the same instant my eye caught sight of a figure some six hundred yards to our right proceeding in the di-rection of the bodies' trenches; and, to crown all, he was a British Tommy!

I thought the man must have gone out of his mind, and when I looked at where he came from, it seemed as if the whole regiment was viewing the daring proceedings of this solitary individual "between the lines." At that part the trenches were much nearer than at ours. They seemed there about two hundred yards apart, while ours were about five hundred yards distant from Fritz.

I saw the solitary Tommy walk right on to within a few yards of the German entanglements and pause a minute; then a boche's head could be seen. At this, Tommy picked his way over the entanglements very cautiously.

My heart was in my mouth! I could scarcely keep from shouting when he reached the edge of the enemy parapet and disappeared!

By this time our regiment was practically all on the fire-step, breathlessly watching and ready for what might hap-pen after the disappearance of this "madcap."

Five minutes more elapsed. Then a head bobbed up at the same spot we had been watching, and out of the trench came the selfsame Tommy. He was carrying something in his hand. My eyes kept steady on him until he reached his own parapet, where he stood a moment flourishing this article; then, clasping it to him as if prizing it, he got down into the trench. While he had stood there for a moment, his fellow trench-mates threw out their arms to take his precious bundle from him, but as I say, he seemed to hold tightly on to it. When I looked back at the place he had just left, the Germans were waving their helmets, with heads above the parapet. It was Christmas all right! and we certainly got a Santa Claus surprise in watching these unusual proceedings.

They were getting bolder on both sides at this part of the line, and a few men began walking on their parapets, finally coming closer and then meeting men from the enemy trench. Then followed a football match with regimental shirts tied up. To see those Tommies charging with their shoulders and explaining the game to the Germans, who were not so well acquainted with it, was a Christmas festival in itself that will never be forgotten by those who witnessed it.

We found out afterward that "Spud" Smith who had just received a lovely "currant bun" from home and was overjoyed with it was jumping round and making so much noise about it, that the fellows dared him to take it over to the Germans and wish them "A Merry Christmas." He at once threw off his equipment and made toward them, where he received his Christmas present in the form of a bottle of "schnapps." "Spud" Smith was the madcap of his regiment.

A few minutes after midnight, we were brought back to war again by the Germans shelling us all along the line.

Everything was tolerably quiet, with the exception of an occasional shelling from either side, until New Year's Eve, when an infernal row got up and on New Year's Day we had about one hundred and thirty casualties. The shelling grew worse, and we discovered that the Saxons had been relieved by the Prussians. Twice they charged us in mass formation, and we were forced to retire to our second-line trenches. It was their idea and intention to break through our lines to get to Calais in time for the Kaiser's birthday. This was the beginning of their big drive. Although we got a severe cutting up, we managed to hold all the ground we had, despite their mass formation, which is a stern and dreadful thing to face.

One morning, about the middle of January, the coal boxes, Jack Johnsons and Black Marias were just simply shaking the earth. The German airplanes had been very active these last few days, and it seemed they were giving their heavy artillery the proper range on our lines. The Jack Johnsons were landing to the right of our regiment and were gradually working their way up toward us. We could see them tearing up parts of the trenches smashing up men, whose limbs were sent flying up through the air. The sight was really too frightful to recall.

Orders were given that the Black Watch should stand to its post and that no man was to retire. But as the heavy shells drew nearer, smashing everything up, they proved too much for the recruits w r ho had joined us only within the last few days, and they made for the reserve trenches. By this time the Germans were beginning to make their advance in waves. Word was passed along that our regiment should retire to its reserve trenches, but it came too late for a few of us, as we were already pumping it into the Germans. Those who had retired were firing over our heads at the advancing Huns, thus making it dangerous for us to withdraw.

Just as I had made up my mind that we must get back somehow, Sergeant Johnstone crept to my side and said;

"Cassells, let's stick it out. This might last only a few minutes more and then it'll be all right again."

"All right, Johnstone," I said; and we shook hands.

Our own shells were bursting so close to our front that they were showering us with earth and stones.

I saw the nearest Germans about a couple of hundred yards away.

Then suddenly a dark curtain dropped before my eyes."

# CHAPTER 14

# Buried Alive

I seemed to awake from a long sleep, only to discover that instead of being in a trench or a billet I was in a hospital; one of the kind made of canvas. There were two great marquee tents, with nurses flitting about quietly like angels they seemed to me, for the moment.

The pain that racked my body was awful. I lay there trying to determine in what part of me the pain was located but it seemed to be all over me. I noticed that either a nurse or an orderly was constantly in attendance at my cot.

As my comprehension of things about me became clearer, I realized that my neighbour was a German. His moaning, coupled with his muttering of *"Ach, mein Gott in Himmel!"* got on my nerves, but I decided to say nothing, as I had not yet learned whether it was an enemy hospital or one of our own. I decided that if it was the former, the quietest way to die was the best, if die I must. During one of the moaning spells of my neighbour, I seemed to lose consciousness. When I "came back," a soft voice whispered in my ear: "It's all right; keep still; we are only taking a plate of your leg."

An English voice! and with such kindness in it! Our own hospital! Not a prisoner! I just wanted to cry out, from sheer happiness.

When next I found myself in my cot, that awful pain was unnerving me, but the doctor, Captain Allen, assured me that I would be all right after a few weeks' rest in Blighty. I immediately asked when I was to go. His reply was:

"When your temperature goes down. It has been 104 for about a week."

I said I would like to write home, and my soft voiced nurse thereupon brought me paper and envelope. I moved to extend my right hand for the paper, and with dismay found it in splints and bandages, with a strong resemblance to a huge boxing glove. Quickly I glanced at the left hand, to find with relief that it, at least, was whole.

I had of course never learned to use my left hand for writing. Observing my need of assistance, the nurse sat on the edge of my bed and took pen and paper to write for me. I had not even to ask her to do this service. The tears came into my eyes at her willing, quiet helpfulness.

After she had finished writing my letter, I asked her about my condition. She seemed reluctant to tell me, but as I urged her to do so she finally said:

"Your leg will probably have to be amputated, as it has been completely turned round and the knee badly shattered. Some splinters of shell still remain in it."

She left me but not for long. She had gone for the plate with the impression of my knee. This she held up to what light could get through the roof of the yellow canvas, and the picture I saw quite startled me. I counted four little black specks around the joint, and to one piece in particular she called my attention. It was about the size of a one carat diamond pointed at both ends and was embedded in the knee cap. This tiny object was giving me nearly all of my pain.

The medical officer on his rounds approached us and greeted me with "You certainly had a miraculous escape."

Later, one of my mates in the hospital, who was with my regiment, told me how I got mine. He had witnessed it. A Jack Johnson striking about fifteen yards in front of the trench I was in, exploded, caving the trench in for a length of about thirty yards. I, with Sergeant Johnstone, who had come up the previous day with reinforcements, was buried completely. Then the Germans charged over the trench at our fellows, who retired to their reserve trenches. However, the enemy was repulsed and had to retire to their own lines again. This fight started about 2 p.m., and it was not until about nine o'clock that night that our company came up and began to re-open the trench. It seems that one fellow was about to use his pick when another close by with a shovel noticed something in the form of a head. He stayed the hand with the pick just in time. It was a head and mine at that. They completely unearthed me, and, as I looked to be dead, placed me to one side with a waterproof sheet over me, to be buried later. Luckily enough, a medical officer examined me and found there was still a little life left. He used artificial respiration, put my legs in splints made up of empty ration boxes, bandaged my damaged right hand, and sent me to the Rouen Hospital, unconscious, but with a spark of life still in me.

Even after two weeks' stay in the hospital my condition was still very critical, but I had the courage and optimism peculiar to the Scot and my hopes for recovery endured stubbornly. The moans of my German neighbour, mixed with cries for *"Das Ei"* didn't allay my fever at all. No one knew what he wanted. Latterly one of our wounded fellows called the nurse over and suggested very earnestly that perhaps he had a glass eye and it needed some attention. The nurse at once examined his eyes, but found them all right.

However, the next medical officer on duty understood

German and acquainted the nurse with the fact that the patient had been calling for an egg. He marked on his chart that he should be given two fresh eggs every morning.

This German was accorded first attention, while our own boys had to be content with being next in line. We could not kick, however, as the doctors and nurses stretched their ability to do for others to the utmost. After our prisoner had had his hunger appeased with the *"Ei,"* he seemed content to die, for that is just what he did. From what I could learn, his injury had been a bad one, a large piece of shell having pierced his chest.

I felt sure, when I saw him carried out, that my turn was next. Then I discovered that the number of my cot was 13, so recalling the many escapes from death I had had and how this number had been concerned in them, my hopes for recovery went soaring high.

Now I was recovering enough to take an interest in other cases in the ward, and one in particular, a Royal Irish Fusilier, in the cot opposite me. He had forty-eight bullet wounds in his body. He had already been in this ward six weeks, so I knew then I wasn't the worst case there. My temperature had now dropped to 100, and I was informed that an orderly would bring my clothes and get me ready for a journey. This meant Blighty!

A couple of the Royal Army Medical Corps men came into the tent and very gently laid me in a stretcher, then carried me out along narrow pathways bordered by neatly whitewashed stones and rows of double-linked marquee tents with similar neat arrangements of stones at the entrances. There seemed to be a city of tents on the Rouen Champ de Course (racecourse), and outside of it too, as far as my eyes could see.

At the end farthest from the cook-house huts, I noticed a large boiler arrangement with a funnel sticking up at one end and on the door some large print, but I could not read the lettering. I asked one of the men what the object was. I was informed that it was used for disinfecting Tommy's clothes and exterminating the cooties that they sheltered. Tommy gets a change to hospital clothing as soon as he enters the base hospital. On taking a second look at the sign, I made out "Germ-Hun Exterminator." So when Tommy gets his clothes out of "dock" (hospital), and grumbles at the R. A. M. C. orderlies when he finds his collection of souvenirs depleted, they promptly put the blame on the "Germ-Hun."

As soon as I was placed in an ambulance, a tag was fastened to my lapel and I was ready for the road along with other lucky chaps. It seemed as if we were hardly settled when we arrived at the railway station. An ambulance train was waiting here for us, and before many minutes had elapsed we found ourselves en route for Le Havre. We arrived here the same night and were placed aboard the S..S. *Asturias*.

When we were about mid-channel, a torpedo from a German submarine just cleared the bow of our ship by a few feet. Even a hospital ship is a target for the missiles of the enemy.

We arrived next morning at Southampton without further occurrences of moment.

Each patient was asked where he wished to be sent. It was natural that each should give his home district. We were placed in rows in the large shed on the wharf, and our destination marked on our tickets. We were now ready for our next part of the journey.

Suddenly my attention was attracted by vigorous exclamations. From the patient in the stretcher next to me I heard vociferous "blimey-ing" in a very strong cockney accent. I asked the disturber what he was making all the row about.

"Blimey," he said, "they've gawn an' gyve me a ticket to th' bloomink end o' Scotland!"

"Is it a mistake?" I asked.

"Mistyke!" said he. "Is it a mistyke? Hit's a mistyke that tykes in th' whole bloomink ge-hography of Britain."

He communed with himself a moment in eloquent but inelegant language. Then he asked:

"Where've they ticketed you to, myte?"

I hadn't thought of looking at my ticket, but now I noted that I was destined for "Chelsea, London, S. W." So he outlined a scheme to which I readily agreed. We exchanged tickets.

I adopted his name "Bill Mortimer" of the Rifle Brigade and soon I was making for "th' bloomink end o' Scotland," while he was en route for Chelsea under his assumed name.

When I arrived in an Aberdeen Hospital, they were a good few days trying to account for me, as my papers had naturally gone to Chelsea. Ultimately they came to the conclusion that there must have been an error at Southampton; and sure enough, my record was finally located at the London hospital.

It was one of the best errors that could have happened, for very soon I found myself in the "Craigleith Military Hospital" within commuting distance of my relatives and friends. I never heard any more of my friend "Bill Mortimer," but I have no doubt the "error" proved a good one to him also.

Two medical officers looked me over very carefully the first day. The next day they came back accompanied by the chief medical officer, Colonel Cottrill. After the latter examined me carefully he said that "an immediate amputation would be the wisest plan." He asked me whether other examining physicians had told me the same thing.

I said: "Yes; but I think it will be all right. See, I can wiggle my toes." And I pointed out that this was a sure sign of hope for a recovery without amputation.

Then commenced a daily routine of bandaging which stretched into months; every conceivable treatment for my betterment was given me; a plaster-of-Paris cast was put on my knee, and after it was on a week or two, the effect was simply wonderful.

By this time, my hand could be used a little, but I found myself minus a finger and with two others broken. They, however, healed to normal.

Every week, during our long stay in the hospital, entertainments were given for us by professional actors and actresses. Visitors were permitted to call Wednesdays and Sundays from 1 to 4 p.m.; on other days from 1 to 3 p.m. I cannot describe the generosity and kindness of the people of Edinburgh.

Every day came armfuls of flowers the most soothing offering a convalescent Tommy can receive, outside of the occasional kiss some dear wee lass would imprint on his cheek. Both are wonderful in their ability to cheer a lonesome Tommy, who, perhaps, finds himself far from his home folk! Every day the ladies and young girls of the town came to sit by our cots and read to us or write our letters. It was an enormous hospital, having often as many as 1100 patients and every man in it, even those who were strangers in Scotland, had daily visitors in plenty. English and Welsh soldiers, too far from home to receive the attention of their own people, were given even more favours than the Scots. Every day, a flock of big motor cars drew up and carried away those who were far enough toward recovery for a ride. We had many delightful hours rolling swiftly through the picturesque city of Edinburgh, along the banks of the Forth and up through the beautiful Pentland Hills.

Our lockers were well filled, and we never wanted for such dainties as chocolates and fancy biscuits, and we had magazines, and above all cigarettes.

A party of our lady visitors brought us wool and volunteered to teach us the art of knitting to while away our idle time. Most of the boys took kindly enough to it, but I wanted to learn embroidery. It caused no end of merriment that a man should want to sew. However, I persuaded them to try me, and one of them offered to do so.

In India I had done quite a little at sketching, and my teacher found me an apt pupil in this allied art. Very soon I had mastered the art of making long and short stitches, French knots, border and buttonhole stitches, etc. I was so highly commended that I received many requests from these ladies for cushion covers, doilies, etc. They brought the materials and I plied the needle. It was such enticing work that very soon two other fellows "joined in."

We had many other ways of passing the time. Visitors would ask us to write or sketch something in their autograph books, which we did with much pleasure, and I can tell you that some very, very funny local sketches and poetry composed on the spur of the moment, with fellow mates, nurses, and doctors as the subjects were carried away from that hospital. They were highly prized by the recipients. We had also a monthly Gazette recording the events of the daily life of the hospital in a breezy and interesting way.

I saw many a bad case brought in, get well, and sent home, but still I remained, and so Corporal Charles Palmer, who had been there the longest, promoted himself to be "Commander-in-Chief" and took me as second in command, I being next to him in length of time there. One of his legs had been blown off six inches above the knee and the pain he suffered at times was excruciating. Another lad, a German, sixteen years of age, had had both legs blown off below the knees by one of the Germans' own shells just as he was about to give himself up to the British. He spoke very good English and was surprisingly cheery. The fair sex found him very attractive and he always got an ample share of the dainties they brought.

I was still in the hospital when the awful "Gretna Green" disaster happened. Perhaps you remember it. A regiment of the Royal Scots was on its way to the front. Their train collided with another at Gretna Green near the Carlisle Junction, resulting in the loss of more than one hundred lives. Some of those that required medical attention were sent to Craigleith, and among the few that found themselves in our ward was a very broad-spoken Scot. He was on seven days' leave, but being "full of happiness," somehow or another got mixed in at Edinburgh station with the lads of the wreck. He spied an empty cot which he immediately made for and fell asleep upon it. Soon afterward, Colonel Sir Joseph Farrer, Commandant of the hospital, came along to see the Gretna lads. When he came to this cot he slowly uncovered the face of the presumed patient and asked:

"How are you?"

The Scot, so rudely aroused, sat up, exclaiming: "Fine, mon; hoo's yersel'?"

The colonel was nonplussed for the moment, but hastily recovered himself however, and shook the extended hand of the erstwhile patient, much to the amusement of the rest of us.

Among the "padres" to visit the hospital was a Major Chaplain of the Church of England. He seemed particularly interested in our ward (G ward) and made as many as three visits a week.

Thursdays, after tea, was prayer meeting for us, as well as for a few of the other wards. Of course, it was impossible for

all the wards to have the meeting on the same evening, owing to the large number of them and the scarcity of clergy-
men, so many of whom were with the boys in France. On
one Thursday evening in particular, the Church of England
chaplain I have just mentioned was about to commence
the service when the absence of the organ (which was a
little portable one, such as is used by the Salvation Army)
was discovered.

A couple of men who could walk volunteered to go in
search of the organ, but they couldn't find it. Then Sister
Brian, a most accommodating nurse, whose Cockney accent was an unmistakable mark of her early upbringing,
went out to locate the missing organ. After a few minutes
she returned and startled the ward by announcing, from the
doorway:

"You men 'ad hall better go to 'Hell' (meaning L ward).
Th' horgan's in 'Hell' an' th' services habout to begin."

There was a general roar of laughter and the reverend
gentleman strenuously refused the invitation.

When the patients were well on the road to recovery,
they would be sent to one of the many mansions opened
by the owners as homes for convalescents. Here they would
remain for a few weeks, perhaps a month, before being
sent to their homes. This stay will be among the pleasan-
test memories of those who experienced it. The beautifully
laid-out and spacious grounds and the auto rides! How it
all helped to hasten recovery!

I cannot conclude without trying to express the praise
which most certainly belongs to the medical officers of
"Craigleith." At the outbreak of the war, Colonel Cottrill
had been retired ten years, but he was found ready when
the first note of the nation's rally sounded, and there he
remained when I left, serving his king and country in
relieving, by his expert skill, the sufferings of those who

come under his care. He was over seventy years of age, but he most truly was seventy years young.

Of the nurses and sisters I could not say enough. Sister Lauder, for instance; I have seen her do thirty-six hours' duty at one stretch, without the slightest rest, at a time when streams of wounded were pouring in day and night. Once she collapsed in the middle of the ward. Such devotion, such wonderful spirit these women exhibited!

I was discharged on August 5th, 1915, being "no longer physically fit for war service.

# CHAPTER 15

# Ned MacD's Story

On a day in February, 1916 a week prior to the sailing of the S.S. *Tuscania*, on which I had taken passage to the United States I had left the office of the Anchor Line and was proceeding up the High Street, of Cowdenbeath (across the river from Edinburgh), bent on an errand pertaining to the preparations for my departure, when I noticed across the way something familiar in the appearance of a tall man in khaki. Twice or thrice I gazed at him, with a sense of dim recollection, and then I went walking or, rather, limping on my way. There were uniforms everywhere and one, even though it seemed in some way distinctive, could not hold my attention. I started to cross the street but when I was in the car track, in the middle, a sound arrested me.

"Reuter! Reuter!" called a voice which was strangely familiar.

Who, thought I, is this, calling me by my nickname? I turned and saw the tall soldier whom I had noticed, limping toward me at the best gait his lameness permitted. I perceived that he wore a Black Watch forage cap. As I stood, awaiting his approach, I suddenly recognized him as my chum, Ned MacD; the same Ned whom I had left in a hollow, in a wood, in France, grievously wounded, and who had mysteriously disappeared when I found opportunity to return in search of him.

I had long believed him dead, for his name had appeared in our casualty lists among those of the killed. I was so overcome at seeing him that I stood as one struck dumb. In a moment, however, we were clasped in each other's arms like a couple of bairns, the tears trickling down our faces.

There we stood, speaking to each other as Scots will, in excitement, in the broad Scotch of our childhood days, until a sharp clang awakened us. It was from a tramcar bell. We were standing in the middle of the single line, and completely blocking traffic. Linking our arms together we made for the pavement.

"I'm mighty glad I met ye, Joe," was his first comment. "I've been trying to find out your whereabouts. To think that Fate should have been kind enough to put you in my way, like that; man, it's just grand!"

I told him of my mission in Cowdenbeath.

"Weel, I'm glad I've caught ye in time, ye bounder, cause I dinna think I could have followed ye to the States to make a visit on ye," he said.

By this time I had fully recovered myself and scrutinized him carefully.

"You've got the same smile, Ned, but my how you've grown! You look at least two inches taller than when I saw you last."

"And that I might," he replied; "come on and I'll tell ye all about it."

So we limped into Cook's tea rooms, secured a table in a quiet -corner, and he told me his story. He spoke in a halting manner, for it brought back many of his sufferings, but to me it is so striking that I felt, in finishing the tale of my war experience, you would like to know about a war romance for romance it surely was with as happy an ending as any novelist might conceive. I will tell to you, as nearly as possible in his own words, the remarkable story he unfolded to me.

"Do ye mind when ye left me in the nook after bandaging my wounds?" he asked. "Weel, I lay there thinking and wondering. Ye ken, Reuter, what I was wondering about about ye're coming back; or maybe someone else might find me and take me back to the lines. But no help came. Then I got to thinking of the lass, and I managed to take her letters, as well as a few fags, from my haversack. I smoked the fags one after the other, and read her dear kind words over and over again. My mind kept dwelling on what was to have been our marriage day. Reuter, remember I told ye about it. It was to have been on the 7th of August, and then on account of the war, we put it off until after I should come back.

"And now, I thought to myself, maybe I'll never get back. All sorts of possibilities passed through my mind, and between this and the awful pain that throbbed all over me, I felt like as if I'd go mad.

"It began to get dark and my patience got exhausted. Then the idea came into my head that I could maybe drag myself along with my hands a wee bit nearer our lines. I thought of your promise, Reuter, but I couldn't stay. A few of the lads around me pegged out one after the other, and it made me feel fair frenzied.

"Do ye remember Stanley Stenning, an English fellow of C company? Weel, he crawled out a wee while before me. I've heard since that he was home, but minus a leg, but I haven't heard so far of any of the other wounded fellows that were in the nook with me.

"Weel, to get back to my own experience. It was awful the pain it racked me through and through, as I tried to move ahead by the aid of my hands. I would take a grip on anything I could get hold of and drag myself on a wee bit at a time. I had managed to do about a hundred yards, when I seemed to sense that I had taken the wrong direction, and oh! how weak I was about that time it's past telling. I just simply had to lie there I couldn't drag myself another inch.

"I remember seeing a few bushes about fifteen yards ahead it seemed so far! and at first I wished I could manage to get to them, thinking I might get out of the way of the enemy, should any of them come along. But after a few minutes I decided it was perhaps as well that I was exhausted, because if I got there and should lose consciousness, ye might not find me, and that it was just as weel I was in the open. So I tried to content myself, but it was maddening.

"In dragging myself to this spot I passed here and there one of our lads then again I would make out one of the Camerons and Reuter, they were so still! But I crawled on, and as the vision of the lass came to me, I felt braver, and made up my mind to hold out as long as I possibly could.

"By this time it was night the time seemed to drag so! Then I remember hearing the sound of some one moving about, and I was just in the act of calling for help when the thought flashed through my brain that maybe they were Germans; so I kept still. The sound soon died away. My! how often, since then, I've wished I had called out.

"I lay there wishing and hoping that I might be found before morning, but the hours dragged on. I was growing fainter and fainter, and more feverish.

"At last, I dimly distinguished the presence of a party. Then I saw them turn over some of the dead Highlanders as they came across them, give each a kick, and pass on. By this time I could see they were stretcher-bearers and Prussians, at that. I was already on my back and therefore hoped they would pass me praying all the time that they would, I kept staring up at the stars. The Huns were passing, but it was over my body. The carrier at the front of the empty stretcher stepped over me, but the man in the rear stepped directly on one of my wounded legs. The pain caused me to groan out. At this they halted and spoke, gruffly, in German.

"They took the contents out of my pockets and haversack, opened the stretcher, laid it alongside of me, rolled me very roughly onto it, and picked it up. Every once in a while during the journey to the dressing station which was quite some distance over broken ground, they would stop and drop the stretcher on the ground, which caused me to groan more and more. There were hundreds of wounded Germans at the station.

"Here I was rolled out of the stretcher. I could feel that the pleats of my kilt were soaked with blood. Presently a little insignificant-looking German with spectacles on looked at me, and asked in English: 'What is the nature of your wounds?'

"I told him. He looked at them very hastily, then said: 'You are lucky. They should have been eight inches farther up.' With a grunt he went to attend to the Prussian patients.

"With that, the Hun lying next to me he had been wounded through the arm and foot noticed me and commenced spitting on me and cursing in German. I made no protest. I was too utterly weak and exhausted.

"At last ambulances drew up near by, and the wounded Germans, after having their wounds dressed, were placed in them. My turn came to be carried onto the ambulance, without, however, any attention having been given to my wounds. After a great deal of jolting about, our ambulance drew up near a railway siding, and the German patients were served with some hot coffee, then we were all put on board a train. By this 'time it was daylight. Almost as soon as I was put on the train it began to move off.

"Shortly afterward, a tall, lean German doctor came over and looked at me, then renewed my dressing, which was the first since yours, Reuter. He asked me in broken English if I had had anything to eat. When I answered in the negative, he walked away and looked over the other patients and talked to them. After quite some time, a German orderly came to me with some hot milk and a sandwich of black bread and very bad smelling cheese. I was given the same treatment as the others while on the train. The doctor told me there were more English wounded on the train, but that was all he said. I cannot say how long I was on the train, but at last, after a lot of shunting, it halted, and all the German wounded were taken off.

"An armed guard of two men came in and took their posts beside me. I was given coffee and more black bread and cheese. I was transferred into a sort of truck, the guard being with me. They cut a few buttons off my jacket as souvenirs.

"After another considerable journey, I was put into a motor ambulance, which brought me to my destination. It was dark when I reached this place and I could not see my surroundings. I was carried into a hut-like arrangement, where I found others, German and British soldiers, and some French also.

"I was only a few minutes in this 'hut' when a big fat, over-fed, severe-looking German officer came in and growled out something in a rough voice. A nurse rushed up to his side. He growled out something else, and she immediately went out. In less time than it takes to tell, she came back with what no doubt he had been growling for. It was a sheet of paper and he commenced reading from it. It was to the effect that the English prisoners would not be allowed to disobey any of the officers, soldiers, orderlies or nurses that if they should do so they would be instantly put to death. If they wished to make complaints they were to do so through the orderlies. However, if the complaint should not be a proper and truthful one, the prisoner making it would be liable to be put to death. He also strongly emphasized the fact that if any prisoner was caught attempting to smuggle or write letters, the sentence of death would instantly be imposed on him. At this point he went away.

"My heart sank. I got so homesick and much weaker; my hopes gave out entirely. I had been thinking that, on reaching my destination, I would be allowed to write home; and now?

"I must have lost consciousness, for it was day time when I awoke, to find two doctors examining my legs, with a number of young students standing around me. One of the doctors, an old man, who spoke excellent English, said that both my thighs were badly fractured and that it would be necessary to operate on me the next morning. Then he commenced explaining to the young doctors. After the explanation was over, they all walked away.

"The next morning I was taken to the operating theatre, which had a gallery all 'round packed with young German students. On the floor there were only a nurse, the old doctor who had spoken to me the previous day, and a few attendants. I was lying on a sort of high-wheel stretcher. The young students were laughing and jeering, when suddenly the old doctor turned on them furiously, using some hot German language, and instantly there was quietness. Then a cap was put under my nose.

"When I came out of the chloroform there was a cage arrangement over my legs and I had no pillow for my head. At the moment I thought it was a very mean trick to do me out of it, but after some experience in the hospital I learned that it was to prevent me from getting sick upon recovering from the effects of the anaesthetic.

"There were about eighteen patients and two nurses in the hut where I was. The nurses took turns of night duty week about. The day nurse during my first week there was a very severe and sour-faced creature. She could speak a little English, and I'm sure she did not speak to me more than twenty times, and not once kindly. The night nurse was a woman about forty years of age She could speak only a very little English, but she was pleasant and good-natured. She took more care of me than any of them and would bring me a glass of milk now and again when the guards were not looking. She also informed me that this was the place that students came to, for practising and xperimenting on the wounded prisoners, and added that I would have a lot more operations which I had.

"Conditions became worse as months dragged on. It was now summer of 1915, and still my legs were not allowed to set. One operation followed another. I saw an iron plate with rusty screw nails an inch long, that had been used to patch up my thigh bones. I suffered much physically but worse than that was the mental suffering I experienced, worrying about my folks at home.

"Every other day, young sarcastic doctors would come in, take the splints off, and commence squeezing and turning my broken legs in a painful fashion. Some would shout: 'English swine, why don't you cry out?' but I don't remember doing so when any of them were near me.

"The food got worse and worse toward winter. I got three meals a day. Breakfast consisted of weak coffee and a slice of black bread with some kind of lard spread on it. Dinner was herring bone or potato-peel soup, or ham-bone soup with a slice of heavy potato bread. Supper was a repetition of breakfast except that very often the lard was absent.

"There were two German patients who got the best of attention. I learned though, that they were wounded in the act of deserting, and were to be court-martialled upon recovery. After they were able to sit up they would get a large jug of beer with their midday meal and this was a keen torture to me.

"I became determined to find some way of communicating with my sweetheart and friends at home, to let them know I was still alive. The night nurse told me she expected to go near the firing line for duty, so I asked her if she could try to smuggle out a letter for me so that it would reach my friends. At first, she very positively refused, saying that should the effort be found out, she would be instantly shot, but after I explained my case to her and pleaded with her she brought me a pencil and note paper and watched a chance when all was quiet. She put a screen round me and whispered in my ear to praise the commandant, and the doctors, and write in the brightest manner of everyone there. Thus, she said, the censor might allow the letter to go through.

"While she watched the guards, I scribbled, doing all she told me to. I described the place and commandant something in the following manner:

This is a most beautiful place. I think it's the prettiest hospital in the great German Empire. It is even more elaborate than the wonderful Peterhead sanatorium at home, and the commandant is the nicest old gentleman. The staff, here, is also superior. We get the best of food and plenty of it and all kinds of recreation. Even visitors bring English magazines and treat me like a relative.

"After finishing it, I gave it to the nurse to read. I had written all the sheet could contain. She looked it over and seemed very pleased with it and said that it would pass the censor all right. She sealed it, then affixed a stamp, and hid it away in her dress, promising to post it next morning.

"I thought it was rather neat, my working in the Peterhead prison in Aberdeenshire, as a sanatorium.

"After the nurse's departure, I slept peacefully and with an easy mind, as if a great burden had been lifted from it.

"When the usual batch of sarcastic young German students came next morning and started in jeering at me, I smiled. One of them instantly leaped forward and gave me a stinging blow on the face with his open palm. I managed to contain myself but how I did it, I don't know.

"That same evening, the commandant came in raging. He nearly ate me up, while in the act of producing the letter I had written the previous night. I longed so for the ground to open and swallow me up. He said the penalty for the offence was death. At first I denied that I knew anything about the letter, but he shouted: 'Do you not remember giving the same address upon coming here?'

"I did, only too well.

"After blazing out, on me, he left, cursing in German. I made up my mind that I was doomed, but decided to lie as long as I could on my cot, as I felt that I would no doubt be shot as soon as I was able to get out of bed. That night a big masculine-looking nurse came on duty, and she was a perfect virago.

"I learned with deep regret that the kind nurse was moved perhaps shot. I watched my chance, and at night, when no one had eyes on me, I twisted in such a fashion that my thigh bones could not possibly get a chance to knit together. The agony I suffered was fearful, but I did not care. In the morning my temperature would go up and further operations would follow. I continued doing this for a week or so but at last I could not stand it. I just had to lie still.

"In December I began to get up for a few hours daily. It was torture to me when I tried to move around. I was so very weak and all the muscle and flesh had left my body. I was reduced to almost skin and bone.

"I was not even given a stick to support me. I limped about for a few weeks, then received my uniform and was moved to the prisoners' enclosure, where there were one thousand British prisoners. Like myself, none of these fellows was allowed to write home, and I don't suppose they will be until they are set free. We were crowded into tents. The food was terrible; I have seen pigs get better. But we ate it just the same.

"The next morning after breakfast, we were all marched out to make roads, chop wood, and do all kinds of convict work. Some of the men had a leg off, others had an arm off as well as being otherwise crippled; but they all had to work.

"I wasn't able to keep up with the rest while marching out to the place where I was to work and one of the German guards started poking the butt of his rifle into my ribs. This was his way of making me keep up with the rest of them. I tried hard and finally managed to reach the spot where our men were working. I was given wood to saw.

"I managed to stick to it about half an hour, then I fainted. When I came to myself again a big dirty Prussian was kicking me and telling me to get on with my work. But I couldn't. Upon seeing this, a man from our squad was ordered to wheel me back to camp in a barrow with a German walking alongside with his rifle slung over his shoulder, smoking a long pipe and jeering all the way. I was at once classed as 'worthless'.

"Our officers had to work like the other men, but the

special job given them was road-sweeping. I was given some dirty work to do around the prison camp for a few days, until at last I had to be put in the hospital again on account of weakness. One of my legs was shorter than the other, owing to the manner in which they had practised on me.

"This time I was in the hospital only about two weeks. Then I got my clothes, and the commandant came in and informed me that he got orders to supply six worthless English prisoners from the camp for exchange. 'You are the first on the list' he said. 'You are no good to anybody. You cannot even work for the food you get.'

"I could hardly realize my good fortune. I wept with joy. To think of being sent home as an exchanged prisoner!

"I 'fell in' along with five more fellows, one was stone blind; his face was an awful sight all dark blue as if it had been tattooed. The other four had body injuries. We were placed in a motor truck which conveyed us to a railway station, then we were packed in trucks with a few sentries over us.

"One of the sentries, out of pity, gave one of our men a cigarette. The poor fellow had just lighted it off the stump the sentry was about to throw away, when a German officer rushed forward and knocked it out of his mouth with his glove, and had him taken away at once. The sentry who had given him the fag was ordered to take off his equipment, and two of the German guards marched the British prisoner and German sentry away.

"Two nights later we landed at a port and were marched on to a steamer. I think it was a Dutch boat, as I did not see any Germans on board until we were out at sea, when we were gathered together, and a German staff officer of the navy gave us a lecture.

"He finished up by saying that we were not free of the

German Government until we landed in England, and should any of us disobey while on board, we would at once be sent back to Germany. You may depend upon it that we obeyed.

"After we boarded the boat we were given some Capstan Navy-Cut Cigarettes and got a good meal, the first since I had been taken prisoner. I was so overjoyed that I sat in a corner and did not utter a word until I landed on British soil, then I prayed silently and thanked God for bringing me back to a civilized country. I think there were over six hundred exchanged British prisoners on the same boat.

"When we landed in England, we were taken to a hospital, and those of us who were able to travel were asked if we wanted to go straight home for a few days, and report for medical treatment in our own districts. I think all those who weren't able to do much more than crawl said they preferred to go straight home. Next morning at 8 o'clock I was given two sovereigns and a furlough, pending discharge.

"After receiving the money, I boarded the first train for Auchterarder, where 'the lass' lived. She had opened a millinery business in my absence. The train left at 10 a.m., and I arrived at Auchterarder depot at 8.15 p.m. It was about a mile from the station to Jeanie's house. I wanted to get there as soon as I could, and walking was out of the question. So I managed to coax a teamster to go a little bit out of his way and let me off near her home. I wanted to surprise her, so went on upstairs in her house quietly.'

"As I climbed up I could hear the sound of much merriment coming from the upper rooms. The first thought that struck me was that perhaps she had been already notified and was preparing a surprise for me. Yet it seemed strange, as I had sent no word ahead of me not even a telegram.

"I felt real nervous upon reaching the door, and wondered what I should say on entering it. At last I summoned up courage and opened the door. I stood still. The sight that met me dazed me. I couldn't believe my own eyes.

"In the room there were many young ladies most of them dressed in white. I recognized some of their faces. Jeanie was standing in the centre, dressed as a bride with a bouquet clasped in her arm.

"I was beginning to think that it surely was a most heavenly surprise. But they caught sight of me and it seemed as if -they all made for the farthest corners of the room. They looked at me in what seemed to be terror.

"Jeanie stared at me for a moment. She was very pale. I wondered why she didn't rush forward and greet me as I felt she ought with outstretched arms. At that I started to make for her side. She gasped out 'Ned' and sank to the floor in a faint.

"While I was leaning over her, there was a commotion at the door. I looked around and saw the clergyman enter, with one of my old-time chums dressed as a bridegroom. Upon recognizing me the bridegroom looked bewildered, but the next moment he had recovered himself.; He approached me and shook hands, telling me, with an odd and embarrassed manner that my arrival was timely. He added: 'If you had been delayed half an hour, Jeanie and I would have been married by now. It seems as if Fate has taken a hand in this'.

"He told me that Jeanie had been worrying and was continually talking about me, and that she didn't believe I was dead, although I had been reported 'killed or missing' since September, 1914. He had told her that she was foolish to keep up this thought, and finally had persuaded her to become engaged to him, The date for the marriage was fixed for the night on which I arrived.

"During this time the bride was being attended by some of the other young ladies and had been revived.

"The intended bridegroom went to her side and asked if she still cared for me. Her answer was: 'If he loves me, yes.' He approached me again, asking whether I cared for her still. Oh, I wanted to say how I loved her and how anxiously and hurriedly I had made my way to her on reaching British soil, but I was too overcome for words; I could only nod an assent. Do you know, Reuter, what this old pal did? He withdrew, giving me his place, and he acted as Best Man.

"Since then I've wondered whether, if it had been any other man, he would have stepped aside so. He loved her as I did, no doubt, but it seems she couldn't forget me, no matter how he tried to make her do so; so, realizing all this at the time, he did what he thought would give her the greatest happiness. I had suffered sorely, Reuter, but surely I was well rewarded. The pal who had expected to have my place gave us a hundred pounds as his gift to help us along in business. We were married that same night only three days ago. So you see, Reuter, I lost no time in trying to find you to tell you of my complete happiness."

We left the tea rooms, and I accompanied Ned to the railway station, where he took the train for his home town. As we parted he wished me the best of success in America, and hoped that he would hear of my getting married very soon, for he assured me he was so happy that he wished to know that such happiness was mine also.

I made for home then, and in less than a week's time I was on my way to the States.

Ned's good wishes for me have certainly been fulfilled. I have since married, and it is my wife who has proved my sole inspiration and help in writing this book.

# CHAPTER 16

# The Black Watch & Me

No doubt, if I had been trained in writing rather than in the tactical requirements for service in the British army, I should call this the appendix of my book. I prefer not to do so, having found in my own experience that readers may be inclined to view the appendix in literature as similar to the appendix in surgery something which is unnecessary.

I cannot so regard this chapter. It is to me a component and interesting part of the whole, for it goes to the source of the splendid and unique traditions of the regiment in which I have been privileged to serve as a soldier of my country.

A great deal has been written about the Black Watch. Even poets have been inspired to sing of its deeds in stanzas which are undying. Men of Highland birth, glorying in its history, have set down the facts of its achievements under England's banner. Yet most of these records are composed of dry facts, with no expressed sense of the romantic and the unusual which enter so largely into the history of the most famous fighting organization in the world. And most of them, also, might be written from the viewpoint of a century ago. They do not bring the recital of the achievements of the Black Watch into the atmosphere of to-day, with due regard for the interesting and almost startling effect of contrast.

This thought came to me one day when I was riding on a trolley through one of the busy districts of that part of Greater New York which lies east of the bridged river, and suddenly realized that I was passing over the very ground upon which the Black Watch had its first important engagement in the war of the American Revolution the Battle of Brooklyn. I recalled that on this very spot, where clanging trolleys, quick motor cars and hurrying pedestrians made a confusing rush of traffic, the men of the Black Watch fought, in the fashion of their forefathers, with broadsword and pistol, against the sturdy pioneers whose descendants are now the allies of our nation in a war for world freedom. In the annals of our regiment, the use of the broadsword and pistol in the Battle of Brooklyn is duly recorded, for it was after this engagement that the regiment was required to lay aside these mediaeval weapons a fact which occasioned such discontent among the veterans of the Watch that there was even fear that the Highland stubbornness might manifest itself as markedly in protest as on the occasion in England, in 1743 when the men of the regiment, confronted with orders issued in ignorance of the Highland characteristics and customs, departed quietly, in a body, without the knowledge of their officers, and marched as far as Northampton with the intention of returning to their Highland homes, relinquishing the purpose only when prolonged negotiations had made the facts of the situation plain to their stubborn minds.

On the whole, however, this disposition on the part of the men of the Black Watch could hardly be called surprising, in view of the ignorance regarding the Highland character then prevalent in England. Three years before, King George the Second, having never seen a Scotch Highlander although the Black Watch had already been organized in the Highlands as the Forty-third regiment of the British army asked to have some examples of the race sent to appear before him and his court. Two Highlanders, Gregor MacGregor and John Campbell, appeared in response to the King's command. (A third, John Grant, began the journey to London with them but died on the way.) MacGregor and Campbell gave exhibitions of their dexterity with the broadsword and the Lochaber axe, in the presence of the King and his Court. When they had finished the King gave each a gold guinea as a gratuity. They gave the coins as a tip to the porter, on their departure. The King had not understood that his guests were Highland gentlemen.

Sitting at the window of the house where I now pass the peaceful and uneventful days of the soldier who has fought until wounds incapacitate him for further service afield, I smiled, one day, at another thought in which the past and the present incongruously came into association. From this window, I viewed the populous, close-built residential stretches of Washington Heights, typical of the city life of to-day. And, amid all this, my eye could seek out the very spot where occurred the grimly humorous adventure of Major Murray, most corpulent of the officers of the Black Watch, when the command was fighting against Washington's rebellious patriots. Having to scale the heights which were later to become famous as the habitat of the hardy goats of Harlem, Major Murray was at a great disadvantage because of his weight and girth. "Soldiers, would you leave me behind?" he appealed, pathetically, when he needed assistance. And then his husky Highlanders would boost him upward toward the fray. It was, consequently, in a somewhat breathless and confused condition that the valiant major attained the spot upon the heights where the conflict raged. Rushing forward to close with some antagonist in the Colonials, Major Murray discovered that his only weapon, his dirk, had got twisted behind him in the strenuous struggles of the ascent and that, because of his excessive fatness, he couldn't reach it.

The records of the regiment, at the home station, Perth, state that the major, on this occasion, tore a sword from the grasp of one of three Colonials who attacked him and put all three to flight. With no thought to cast aspersion upon the major's valour, I have always been inclined to the belief that the writer of the regimental reports may have compensated in a certain generosity of statement for his earlier description of the major's comic predicament.

Study of the history of the Black Watch, gathered, largely, in a fragmentary way, has always had a fascination for me. I have felt in the greatest degree the pride of membership in the organization and the world knows that the men of the Black Watch have always made much of the name, I feel that tradition had well prepared the regiment for its sacrificial and almost superhuman efforts between Mons and the Marne. For hard fighting and long fighting in every quarter of the globe and with opponents of almost every race civilized and uncivilized no t organized fighting force has ever had a record to equal that of the Black Watch.

The regiment got its name in 1729, when six companies of Highlanders which had constituted a sort of military police along the highland border, were joined together into a more or less homogeneous command. Four of these companies had been in existence for a few years. Two were of organization of that year. They were called the Independent Companies of Highlanders but it was their purpose to co-operate to preserve order among the turbulent spirits of the border and to enforce the disarming act. Highlanders from the broken clans flocked to the banners of the Independent Companies, as this gave them the right still to bear arms. Many of them were Highland gentlemen, who came with their servants to carry their arms and belongings. The companies were commanded by Lord Lovat, Campbell of Lochnell, Grant of Ballindalloch, Campbell of Fonab, Campbell of Carrick, and Munro of Culcairn. Approximately, there were a hundred men in each company. They wore the dark tartan of the clan Campbell, and thus came to be called the *Freaceadan Dubh*, or Black Watch, as distinguished from the *saighdearan dearg*, or red soldiers.

For ten years, these six companies served on the border, constituting a slender but effective bulwark between two neighbouring but utterly different peoples. In this day when it is but a pleasant outing to motor from England into the Highlands it seems almost unbelievable that the laws, language, customs, and social usages of the Highlanders should for centuries have remained utterly different from those of England and the lowlands, and that the people of the lowlands should have almost no knowledge of neighbours so near. The sturdy and soldierly qualities of the Highlanders of the six companies, however, couldn't escape the notice of England's generals, ever seeking new drafts for England's fighting forces.

In 1739 it was decided that a foot regiment of Highlanders should be added to the regular establishment of the army, the six Independent Companies being augmented by four new companies to constitute the regimental strength.

In 1740 this regiment commanded by the Earl of Crawford and Lindsay, as colonel, was paraded for the first time on a field, near Aberfeldy. Until then, the Black Watch had been uniformed only in the fact that each member wore the *philleadh mor* or belted plaid, of the Campbell tartan. No one but a Highlander could ever adjust this dress. It consisted of twelve yards of tartan, two thirds of it gathered in pleats, held by a belt round the waist, and the other third folded around the body and clasped with a buckle, on the left shoulder.

The uniform and individual equipment of the new regiment, which was called the Fortythird Foot, is described in detail in an old order of the day. It consisted of "scarlet jacket and waistcoat, with buff facings and white lace; the *phileag beag*, or little kilt; a blue bonnet, with check border of red, white, and green, and a tuft of feathers; musket, bayonet, pistol, broadsword, dirk and target." The first march of the regiment was from beside the waters of the Tay where it had encamped for more than a year to Perth, in which city the home station of the regiment was then established and still is maintained.

When I outfitted there, with my contingent of first reserve men, at the outbreak of this war, the thought came to my mind that, three times before, the Black Watch had moved from Perth to fight in Flanders.

I have never seen a succinct summary of the activities of the Black Watch. Though far abler writers than I have described its separate campaigns, each of these writers has given but a limited view of the long vista of sturdy fighting which visualizes the regiment's history. From such sources of information as I have had, the following summary has been extracted. Surely it will tell a story of interest to every man who is interested in the traditions of Britain's "far-flung battle line."

The regiment marched from Perth to London, in 1743, and, after a mutiny due to tales of scandal-mongers that the Highlanders were to be sent to the American plantations, made its first journey overseas, going to fight in Flanders under the command of the Earl of Stair. After Fontenoy, the regiment covered the British retreat and lost, among their officers, five Campbells. In this battle they were commanded by Sir Robert Munro.

The Black Watch, then called the 43rd Highlanders, was transferred to England, and most of the companies were kept in Kent, during the Jacobite uprising. Three companies were engaged in Scotland in putting down the insurrection, and one was at the battle of Prestonpans. I quote from a story of the Black Watch written by Lauchlan MacLean Watt in saying that "the other two companies had an unwilling share in the deplorable outrages in the Highland Glens after Culloden, which made the name of the Duke of Cumberland worthy to be placed amongst those of his blood who have won similar distinction in Belgium, to-day."

The Black Watch was sent to France, in 1746, thence to Ireland and back to Flanders in 1747.

In 1749 it was returned to Ireland where it remained eight years. In this year the regimental number was changed to the 42nd.

In 1757 the regiment was a part of the expeditionary force sent to America for the French and Indian war. At Ticonderoga it served so valiantly and suffered such terrific losses that the name "The Royal Highlanders" was conferred upon it.

The regiment next fought at Martinique and Guadaloupe, returning to fight again in Canada and take an important part in the battle which compelled the surrender of Montreal. Altogether, it served seven years in the West Indies and North America. It was only at this period that company sergeants were given carbines instead of the Lochaber axes which they had always carried.

In 1775 the regiment returned to Scotland, having been absent 32 years.

In April, 1776, the regiment embarked again for America, this time to fight in the revolution of the American colonists. They were disembarked on Staten Island, and, as I have said, they were engaged and suffered some losses in the Battle of Brooklyn. They also suffered heavily in the Battle of the Brandywine.

The Black Watch next fought against Hyder Ali, in India, in 1782.

In 1795 it took part in the defence of Nieuport, in Flanders, and suffered much in the Gildersmalsen retreat, in that campaign.

Back again, the regiment went, after this, to the West Indies and in this campaign the men were first given a uniform suitable to wear in the tropics. Its principal features were white duck trousers and round hats. The mutations of world warfare had had their effect. The Highlanders were willing to put on pantaloons. There were but five companies of the regiment on this expedition. The whole regiment was reassembled, however, in the following r year, at Gibraltar, and fought as a whole in the capture of Minorca.

The year 1800 found the regiment, under Sir Ralph Abercromby, in Egypt. During the fighting with Napoleon's armies, there, the regiment lost its commander in action.

In 1808 the Black Watch was among the British forces in the Peninsula and suffered extreme privation and heavy losses on the retreat from Corunna.

In the following year the regiment was on the ill-fated expedition to Walcheren, returning with less than one-third of its original strength. Three years later they were in Portugal again.

After the escape of Napoleon the regiment fought through to Waterloo, though without playing an important part in that last great battle.

It then fought through the campaign of the Crimea as a part of Sir Colin Campbell's Highland brigade.

Within a year it was in the lead of the force of six thousand men which Sir Colin led against twenty-five thousand mutineers at Cawnpore.

Its next hard fighting was in the Ashanti campaign, under General Sir Garnet Wolseley.

In 1881 it was combined with the 73rd Highland regiment (formerly the 2nd battalion of the Black Watch) and in the next year was back, fighting in Egypt. Through the whole of that war in Egypt it was in the forefront, fighting with distinction up to the end of the expedition which was organized for the relief of Gordon at Khartoum.

The regiment suffered its most terrific losses up to those of the retreat from Mons in the South African campaign. The slaughter of the Black Watch, at Magersfontein, when the Boers ambushed it in close formation, was the most shocking news that came to England from the Cape.

The story of the 2nd Battalion of the regiment and its deeds is a separate one, through several decades. It sailed to India in 1780 and was in action in all of the big and little Indian wars of that early and troublesome time. In 1809 it was made a separate regiment and called the 73rd Highlanders. As such it served at Waterloo, and it remained a separate unit until 1881, when it was reunited with the original 1st Battalion.

The Black Watch, as now organized, might almost be called a small army. There is a depot battalion at Perth, four territorial battalions in Scotland and six service battalions.

In 1905, I enlisted in the 1st Battalion of the Black Watch the same "Royal Highlanders" that had won its designation at Ticonderoga. In 1907, I was transferred to the 2nd Battalion, which had been known as the 73rd Highlanders. I joined them at their station at Peshawar, near the mouth of the famous Kyber Pass, in Afghanistan. In the athletic contests for which the regiment was famous, I met as a competitor, Ned MacD, the same Ned MacD whose romantic story I have told in a previous chapter. After a time we were the regimental champions, and, many a day in India, we strenuously upheld the honour of the Black Watch in competition with the men of other regiments.

My athletic days and my fighting days are over. But ever my blood will quicken with the thought that I have played my part and done my service and shed my blood in the ranks of the Black Watch, fighting for Right and for the Freedom of Mankind. The pain of old wounds will ever vanish, the regrets for departed comrades will ever fade into forgetfulness when I read, again, the verses which paraphrase the title conferred by the bodies upon the Black Watch upon us!

# 'The Ladies from Hell'

There's a toss o' th' sporran,
A swing o' th' kilt,
A screech frae th' pipers
In blood-stirrin' lilt;
They step out together
As pibroch notes swell
Oh, they're bonny, braw fighters,
"The ladies from Hell."

They're far frae th' heather
An' far frae th' moor;
As th' rocks o' their hillsides
Their faces are dour.
Oh, "Th' Campbells are Comin'
Frae corrie an' fell
What a thrill to their slogan!
These "Ladies from Hell."

As they charged at Culloden
Like fire o'er th' brae,
Their brothers are charging
In Flanders to-day.
One lesson in manners
The boche has learned well:
'Tis: Make way for the ladies
"The Ladies from Hell."

LEONAUR

# ALSO FROM LEONAUR

**AVAILABLE IN SOFTCOVER OR HARDCOVER WITH DUST JACKET**

**SEPOYS, SIEGE & STORM** *by Charles John Griffiths*—The Experiences of a young officer of H.M.'s 61st Regiment at Ferozepore, Delhi ridge and at the fall of Delhi during the Indian mutiny 1857.

**CAMPAIGNING IN ZULULAND** *by W. E. Montague*—Experiences on campaign during the Zulu war of 1879 with the 94th Regiment.

**THE STORY OF THE GUIDES** *by G. J. Younghusband*—The Exploits of the Soldiers of the famous Indian Army Regiment from the northwest frontier 1847 - 1900..

**ZULU: 1879** *by D.C.F. Moodie & the Leonaur Editors*—The Anglo-Zulu War of 1879 from contemporary sources: First Hand Accounts, Interviews, Dispatches, Official Documents & Newspaper Reports.

**THE RECOLLECTIONS OF SKINNER OF SKINNER'S HORSE** *by James Skinner*—James Skinner and his 'Yellow Boys' Irregular cavalry in the wars of India between the British, Mahratta, Rajput, Mogul, Sikh & Pindarree Forces.

**TOMMY ATKINS' WAR STORIES 14 FIRST HAND ACCOUNTS**—Fourteen first hand accounts from the ranks of the British Army during Queen Victoria's Empire Original & True Battle Stories Recollections of the Indian Mutiny With the 49th in the Crimea With the Guards in Egypt The Charge of the Six Hundred With Wolseley in Ashanti Alma, Inkermann and Magdala With the Gunners at Tel-el-Kebir Russian Guns and Indian Rebels Rough Work in the Crimea In the Maori Rising Facing the Zulus From Sebastopol to Lucknow Sent to Save Gordon On the March to Chitral Tommy by Rudyard Kipling

**CHASSEUR OF 1914** *by Marcel Dupont*—Experiences of the twilight of the French Light Cavalry by a young officer during the early battles of the great war in Europe.

**TROOP HORSE & TRENCH** *by R. A. Lloyd*—The experiences of a British Lifeguardsman of the household cavalry fighting on the western front during the First World War 1914-18.

**THE EAST AFRICAN MOUNTED RIFLES** *by C. J. Wilson*—Experiences of the campaign in the East African bush during the First World War.

**THE FIGHTING CAMELIERS** *by Frank Reid*—The exploits of the Imperial Camel Corps in the desert and Palestine campaigns of the First World War.

www.ingramcontent.com/pod-product-compliance
Lightning Source LLC
Chambersburg PA
CBHW021110090426
42738CB00006B/589